Gardener's Handbook 2
Conifers

Gardener's Handbook 2

Conifers

David Carr

B. T. BATSFORD LTD, LONDON

First published 1979
© David Carr 1979
ISBN 0 7134 1307 7 cased
ISBN 0 7134 1308 5 limp

Filmset in VIP Times by Elliott Bros. & Yeoman Ltd.,
Speke, Liverpool L24 9JL
Printed by The Anchor Press, Tiptree, Essex
for the publishers B. T. Batsford Ltd,
4 Fitzhardinge Street, London W1H 0AH

Contents

List of colour plates

1   A group of conifers in subtle shades of green, blue and gold, with a blue Cedar in the background and *Thuya* 'Rosedalis' in the centre

2   An element of seasonal change is afforded by using broad-leaved trees for soft shades of spring green

3   The fastigiate Irish Juniper, flanked by conical varieties of *Chamaecyparis*

4   Summer interest provided by heathers interplanted with a ground-hugging Juniper and green fastigiate and gold conical conifers

5   A study in blue and gold in late summer or autumn – blue Spruce with golden Cypress

6   A late summer scene with *Juniperus conferta,* Lawson Cypress and a blue *Cedrus atlantica glauca*

7   The startling effect of blue Spruce amongst conifers in the weak winter sunshine

Colour transparencies supplied by kind permission of Harry Smith, horticultural photographic collection

List of conifers

Botanical names

English popular names

American popular names

Introduction

This volume is designed to complement Gardener's Handbook 1, *Broad-leaved Trees*, and it is arranged in a similar manner. The aim is to give practical guidance on the use, selection and care of garden conifers.

The diminishing size of new gardens means that the wise selection and use of conifers is perhaps of greater importance than ever before. But the unwary garden owner may easily be tempted to purchase trees unsuitable for the intended purpose.

While there are numerous books on the general subject, much of the information is either fragmented or rather specialized.

This book is divided into two sections. The first part is devoted to the use, planting and care of conifers. This provides basic facts of general cultivation, information essential to a gardener if he is successfully to plant and care for conifers. In the second part details are given of the appearance, requirements, care and use of individual conifers suitable for planting in gardens. This should simplify the task of selecting the right trees for a site.

Conifers and their characteristics

Conifers form a large group of woody, mainly cone-bearing plants, most of which, but not all, are evergreen. The majority of conifers originate in the temperate and sub-arctic regions, often almost on the snow line on hills and mountains. Many of these plants are very hardy. Conifers are of diverse habit of growth and in ultimate size they range from diminutive dwarf specimens to the tallest trees known. They often have narrow, needle-like leaves or leaf scales. Although leaf fall and new growth are less obvious than with decidous trees, the colours of the foliage vary considerably according to the time of year.

The garden use of conifers

Many people, when conifers are mentioned, have visions of dark forests of green, unrelieved by other colours or forms of vegetation. However, conifers can play an important role in the well designed garden, irrespective of size. They can provide interesting colours, shapes and forms not supplied by any other plants. Some notable garden designers have suggested that in order to ensure foliage, colour and interest at all times of year half to two-thirds of any planted area should consist of evergreens. Part or all of an area of evergreens may be devoted to conifers, which can be obtained in many shapes, sizes and colours.

Narrow, upright conifers can be used to provide shelter, screens and wind protection, where spreading broad-leaved trees might be unsuitable for reasons of size or winter bareness.

Small conifers and dwarf forms can be fitted into small gardens with comparative ease. These offer great opportunities to a skilful garden designer, but the novice should avoid the pitfall of placing, say, a 600mm (2ft) pygmy too close to a large forest tree. Dwarf forms can be used in rock gardens, and under other trees as ground cover. Some varieties are excellent for hedging and screening purposes, as well as providing a background for colourful planting schemes.

Planting conifers

The art of good cultivation consists of: correctly assessing the various aspects of a site, its climate and soil; then choosing plants to suit both site and intended purpose; and, finally, by good cultural practice, ensuring that plant needs are met.

Factors which influence plant growth and development in any garden are: climate; soil; biological influences; time; and the attention of the cultivator.

Conifers of one type or another are suitable for almost every planting purpose that can be imagined. There are trees in this group which can be planted in shade or sun, in wet or dry sites, on acid or alkaline soils. Conifers may be planted singly as specimens or in groups, either alone or among shrubs and heathers, to provide height and form in planting schemes.

Climate

Climate, by which I mean here the combined and cumulative effects of sun, rain, wind and frost, imposes certain characteristics on an area and its vegetation.

Plants and trees are described as hardy when and where they can survive normal winters outdoors without serious harm. Those which are quite hardy in a mild climate may not survive the rigours of harsh conditions and severe winters. On a smaller scale, in a sheltered garden a tree may survive severe weather unharmed while another of the same variety in an exposed position in the same neighbourhood is less fortunate.

Soils

Soils vary in their chemical and physical composition, and conifers, like other plants, show certain preferences for particular soil types. However, conifers are on the whole less demanding than broad-leaved trees as regards soils.

Fertile soils contain essential plant nutrients, including nitrogen, phosphates, potash and other elements. They are also free-draining.

One of the most important single factors influencing growth is soil reaction, which can be expressed or measured against the pH scale. Soils having a pH level of 7 are neutral, those below are acid, and those above are alkaline. The presence of chalk or limestone is usually indicative of neutral or alkaline conditions.

The physical qualities of soil vary greatly according to the relative quantities of sand and clay present. Clay soils are sticky and heavy when wet, and rock-hard when dry. Sandy soils are gritty to the touch, free-draining, and easier to cultivate. The most productive soils consist of well balanced blends of clay and sand, suitably manured, fertilized and limed as necessary.

Biological influences

Plants and animals act and react with each other to influence growth and development. In a natural wood, for example, there are often thin, narrow, spindly trees which because of the unequal competition with others have not been able to develop properly. In a garden it is important to allow trees adequate space to grow and develop.

Again, if we consider the levels of vegetation in a woodland setting, there are at least three or four. Trees provide the topmost canopy, and the amount of light that reaches the lower levels will affect the nature and extent of the undergrowth. The lowest layers of vegetation consist of the woodland floor plants, which roughly correspond to the herbaceous plants, grasses and heathers of gardens. The intermediate layer of scrub, between floor and overhead canopy, has its counterpart in garden shrubs. Each of these layers competes against the others for food, light and moisture, a factor to be considered when planting. Last, but by no means least among plants, are members of the micro-flora – the mosses, lichens, fungi and others. Some of these live by growing on our cultivated plants and cause disease, but others live in symbiosis, usually on or in the roots, and are essential for the well-being of some conifers and other plants.

Birds and animals, especially members of the insect world, can also exert considerable influence on the success or failure of our trees. Caterpillars, which devour vast quantities of leaves, are among the most destructive, and steps to control them are occasionally necessary.

Time
Time is a very significant dimension, especially where the cultivation of trees is involved. When dealing with trees we are concerned with plants not only in the present but for some years ahead, changing and growing in size and stature. A point which needs particular consideration is the ultimate height and spread in relation to the surroundings, not forgetting the depth and breadth of the root systems.

Figure 1
Tree size
Left to right: young, part-grown, and mature tree – note root spread relative to house foundations as well as diameter (D)

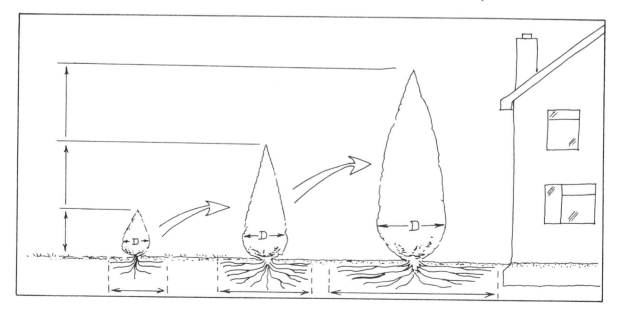

The attention of the cultivator
The aims of a good gardener should be: to select and plant the tree or trees best suited to a site; to provide good growing conditions; and to attend to the needs of plants, training and pruning as and when

necessary. Factors affecting the selection of trees are considered in detail in the sections on individual conifers in the second part of the book. But before considering the nature and methods of the cultural operations involved in tree growing, some indication of tree requirements may be helpful.

Requirements for growth
Each of the factors listed below plays an important role in the life of a conifer. Some of these we can control, others we can influence only to a limited extent.

Temperature is one of the most powerful factors – growth of most hardy trees ceases for practical purposes below about 6°C (42°F) and increases rapidly with greater warmth above that level. The precise level at which low temperatures damage plants/trees depends on their hardiness, the season, and their condition. Conifers are usually hardier than broad-leaved trees.

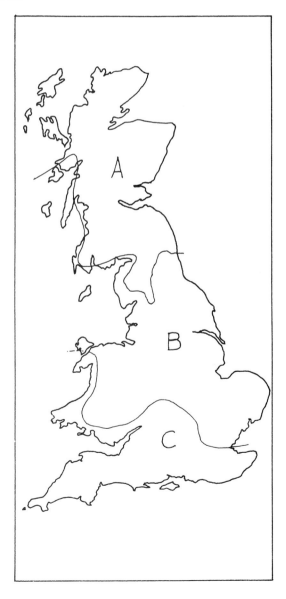

Figure 2
Climate zones
United Kingdom, excluding
Northern Ireland

13

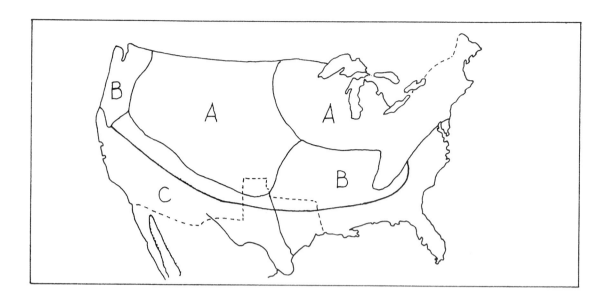

Figure 3
Climatic zones
United States of America

Conifers can be classed in descending order of hardiness, A, B and C, which relate to climatic zones (Figures 2 and 3).

Water, especially soil moisture, and air are of the utmost importance to the survival, growth and development of trees.

Too much or too little water can be fatal. Roots can extract essential plant nutrients from the ground only when they are dissolved in a dilute watery solution. Excess water for long periods results in suffocation of tree roots and death.

Sunlight is vitally important to trees and their development. Light is, of course, necessary for plants to manufacture sugars and starches by means of chlorophyll in their leaves, without which growth would cease. But as not all sites are in full sun, it is necessary to know which varieties either need or can tolerate light shade.

Another important requirement is adequate space to grow. Overcrowding results in weak, spindly disease-prone growth. The roots of trees which are planted too close to buildings and drains can damage foundations and cause blockage.

Finally it is important to consider the effects of pollution, especially when planting in towns. Pollution in towns takes many harmful forms: sulphur deposits, which cause soil acidity; salt spray from roads; fumes and deposits affecting plant processes. Evergreens, and conifers in particular, are less able to tolerate high levels of pollution than deciduous trees – an important consideration when selecting trees for planting in towns.

Selecting conifers
In selecting a conifer several points have to be taken into consideration. What kind of tree is wanted? Will that tree grow where it is intended? What are the requirements of the tree or trees for best results? Last but by no means least, what is the correct name of the tree we want?

In present-day gardens, trees, other than those grown for fruit, are required primarily for decorative purposes, but also serve to provide shelter and screening. When selecting trees for screens, take care to choose a variety that is sufficiently hardy for the purpose in mind. For example, in an exposed position wind can cause disfiguration of tender trees.

The shape or outline of trees can provide considerable scope for variety and interest in any garden layout. There are several basic forms or outlines of conifer habit, and these are briefly discussed below.

Columnar trees are tall and narrow in proportion to their height. The Incense Cedar is an example of this type. Fastigiate trees are similar to, but have more ascending branches than columnar forms. Pyramidal forms are conical in outline, broader at the base, narrowing and tapering towards the top. The majority of conifers are in this group

Globose or round-headed forms are often found among coniferous trees. Many dwarf conifers are examples of this group.

Upright trees: while most of these grow upright, trees so described have near vertical sides for most of their height. The type, such as some Yews, grows roughly twice as high as broad.

Another basic type consists of weeping forms. These are less common among conifers than among broad-leaved trees; however, Brewer's Weeping Spruce is an example.

Procumbent forms of conifers are common. These can be prostrate, growing close to and spreading over the ground. Intermediate or semi-prostrate types also occur.

Other important considerations are colour and season of interest. Conifers can provide year-round colour with their foliage, and so are valuable for winter interest. Some conifers also produce attractive cones which, while less colourful than some fruits or berries, have a charm of their own. Some indication of these features is given where appropriate.

Buying conifers

This aspect of selection should include some thought about the size and condition of tree being obtained. This in turn depends to some extent on the planting season.

Most are, for best results, planted in early autumn or late spring, when the soil is warm and moist to encourage quick establishment.

When selecting conifers, choose specimens which are of good shape, and well covered or furnished with foliage from base to top. Avoid those which have lost the lower leaves and show bare stems. Conifers rarely regain lost foliage, especially near the base.

The forms in which trees can usually be obtained are summarized in the following list.

Transplants: young nursery stock, with either a single stem or a number of short growths or shoots. These can vary in height from about 100mm (4in.) to 450mm (1½ft). However, this form does require pruning to produce a good shape, and to restrict the vertical stems to a central leader where necessary.

Small trees: conifers in particular are best moved when fairly small, usually 300–900mm (1–3ft) high.

15

Two other forms of tree are sometimes offered for sale.

Extra-heavy nursery stock: trees which have been grown on for an extra year or two and have a better developed framework of branches and roots, as well as thicker stems. This grade is usually confined to container-grown trees.
Semi-mature, large trees: occasionally available, but their high cost, and, in the case of conifers, much lower chances of success, do not make them a particularly attractive proposition. Their chief advantage is immediate effect.

Trees can be prepared in the following ways as regards treatment of the roots.

Bare-root plants: with all the soil removed. This treatment is adequate for some varieties of conifers, provided they are small trees; do not dry out; and are lightly pruned immediately after planting. Balled plants: with a ball of soil around the roots.
Balled-and-wrapped plants: with the root ball wrapped in hessian or similar material, to prevent the soil from working loose and drying out. This method, when carefully carried out, works well for most kinds of conifer. Container-grown plants: grown in pots or some kind of receptacle. Conifers so treated can be planted out at almost any time of year, provided the ground is not frozen, waterlogged or baked hard.

Naming and labelling

The wrong naming or labelling of trees is not only frustrating and infuriating, but can be costly in time and money. Trees are a long-term venture, and it is rather too late to discover after five or ten years that you have the wrong variety.

The naming of conifers understandably causes confusion, and this can lead to somewhat strained relations between buyer and seller. The varieties of some conifers differ widely in both foliage and shape. Some conifers, such as Juniper, have juvenile foliage until a certain point in their life cycle is reached, and then assume adult foliage. A few even have intermediate forms.

Many conifers do not have popular names, which can in any case be misleading, and so the convention of botanical naming is usual. This need not be so daunting as it at first appears. The system is really rather similar to that used when recording the names of people on official forms, when the family or surname comes first. In the case of trees or plants the 'generic' name or genus is first. The second name, the species or specific name can be thought of as a Christian name. The third and subsequent names are reserved for the variety. In the case of plants raised or selected in gardens the term 'cultivar' is used to differentiate them from varieties found in the wild. As an example of this botanical convention, take *Cedrus deodara* 'Aurea'. *Cedrus* is the generic or genus name. *Cedrus deodara* is the name of the species. *Cedrus deodara* 'Aurea' is the name of the variety, or, more correctly, the cultivar.

This tree provides a convenient illustration of the importance of giving the full name. *Cedrus deodara,* the species, can grow to an ultimate height of 75m (245ft), though it infrequently exceeds 12–15m

(40–50ft) in cultivation. It has grey-green foliage. *Cedrus deodara* 'Aurea', the cultivar, is unlikely to exceed 5m (17ft) maximum, and it has golden yellowish green foliage.

The following table sets out in summary form the factors to be borne in mind when choosing trees for a garden.

Figure 4
Conifer habit
Left to right: columnar; globose or round; weeping; spreading, flat-topped shrub; spreading, flat-topped tree; pyramid; procumbent; and broad columnar

Tree habit

1 Columnar		
2 Pyramidal		
3 Globose or round	any of which can	
4 Upright	be combined with the	
5 Weeping	following permutations	
6 Procumbent, spreading		

Tree form
1 Transplants
2 Small trees
3 Extra-heavy stock
4 Semi-mature trees

Tree root condition
1 Bare root
2 Balled
3 Balled-and-wrapped
4 Container-grown

Other considerations
Purpose of planting
Ultimate size: height, width and rootrun
Rate of growth
Nature of interest: leaves, flowers, fruits, etc.
Season of colour
Needs of conifers: site and soil
Hardiness
Cultural requirements, pruning and training
Correct naming and identification

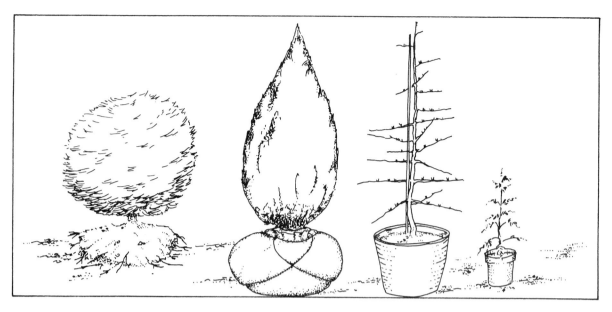

Figure 5
Planting material
Left to right: balled conifer;
balled-and-wrapped c.; container-
grown c,; and pot-grown c.

Cultural requirements

For best results cultivations should be carried out in a logical sequence. If we take as our starting point an uncultivated site, the sequence of operations can be considered under a number of stages.

Site preparation

First, the ground should be cleared of all weeds and rubbish. Dig out perennial weeds like docks, nettles and thistles. Where land is choked with weeds it is better in the long term to defer planting and apply weedkiller, so as to be able to start with clean ground. Suitable weedkillers for use on vacant land include, for use against most herbaceous weeds and grasses: atrazine; bromacil; sodium chlorate with fire depressant; and 2,4–D. Brushwood is best cleared by digging and burning. Where honey fungus is present or suspected old tree stumps should if possible be dug up and burnt, and soil in the vicinity of affected plants should be drenched with a 2 per cent formaldehyde solution. With all these substances care should be taken to avoid spillage or spraydrift on garden plants, and the ground should be clear of harmful chemical residues before plants are set out. The time the soil needs to be left before planting depends on rainfall, soil type, and the nature and amount of the herbicide or sterilizing solution used. Follow the makers' instructions.

Where water is slow to drain, or lies on the soil surface for long periods, the land drainage should be checked and corrected. The soil should be improved by incorporating manure, sand or other coarse material to dispose of surplus water, and the installation of land or pipe drains or a soakaway sump should be considered.

Any changes to ground levels should be made before planting, when it is both quicker and easier.

The area around the immediate planting excavation should be dug to a spade depth, especially where levels have been lowered. Incorporate some manure or similar material at the same time as digging.

Preparations for planting

For a single tree excavate a hole at least 600mm (2ft) square and as deep. Where a large root ball is being planted, increase the size to at least 300mm (1ft) wider and deeper than the size of the root mass.

Fork up the bottom of each hole, incorporating one bucketful of peat or well rotted manure plus 120g (4oz.) of bonemeal to each 600 × 600mm (2 × 2ft) hole. Increase the quantities proportionately for larger holes.

Figure 6
Planting preparation
Left: test hole for size
Centre: fork peat into the bottom and mix some with the soil for filling
Right: hammer in stake, where necessary, before planting

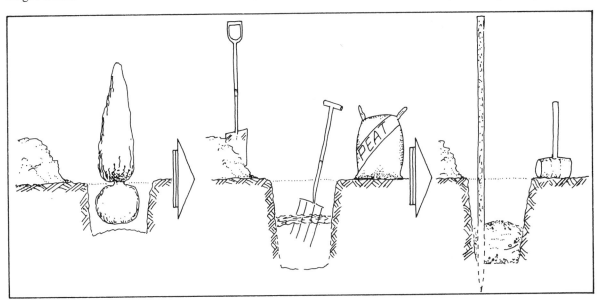

Where conifers are to be planted closely in beds instead of singly, double dig the whole area. Incorporate manure or peat and bonemeal at the same rate to the whole bed.

Hammer in a suitable support where necessary, before planting. Timber stakes should be debarked and treated with an approved safe preservative. The stake, say 40mm (1½in.) square for a tree over 1.2m (4ft) or a stout cane if less, should be of sufficient length so that the top reaches about three-quarters to two-thirds the way up a small tree when the bottom is buried about 300mm (1ft) below the base of the root ball.

Mix good topsoil (the excavated topsoil where this is of reasonable quality) with peat and sand in the ratio of, parts by volume, five parts soil to two parts peat and one part sand. Add 60g (2oz) of balanced fertilizer per bucketful, mixing all together very thoroughly.

Spray container-grown plants with an anti-wilting preparation before planting in hot and dry weather.

Planting

Conifers which are not in containers and which are delivered well in advance of planting must not be allowed to dry out, and are best heeled-in until it is possible to plant them. Heeling-in consists of digging a hole of sufficient depth, placing the roots in it and covering them with soil. Any roots which have dried out in transit should be soaked in water for several hours before being set out.

Avoid planting when the soil is frozen, baked dry or waterlogged.

Programme for care of conifers

Task	When to be carried out			
	Spring		Late	spring
Apply weedkiller to vacant land	X	X	X	X
Level vacant land	X	X	X	X
Check/install drainage	X	X	X	X
Apply/spread manure	X	X	X	X
Dig/fork/cultivate ground	X	X	X	X
Spread lime when necessary	X	X	X	X
Final preparations for planting	—	X	X	X
Prepare space for heeling-in	X	X	X	X
Heel-in trees	X	X	X	—
Plant bare root or b-a-w conifers	—	—	X	X
Plant container-grown conifers	—	X	X	X
Inspect, erect, renew, adjust tree stakes/ties	X	X	X	X
Provide temporary shelter for young conifers	X	X	X	X
Water and syringe newly planted trees	—	X	X	X
Apply mulch around trees	X	X	X	X
Surface cultivation	X	X	X	X
Firm newly planted trees after frost/wind	X	X	X	X
Weed	X	X	X	X
Apply top dressing	X	X	X	X
Examine/repair temporary tree shelter	X	X	X	X
Encircle tree with cord/ fix to keep conifer shape	X	X	X	X
Dislodge heavy snow resting on trees	X	X	X	—
Place tree guards around conifers	X	X	X	X
Cut dead/diseased wood out of trees	X	X	X	X
Trim/shape conifers	—	—	X	X
Undercut conifers to be moved	—	X	—	—
Take cuttings	—	—	—	—
Layer branches	—	X	X	—
Carry out grafting	—	X	X	—

Summer		Late summer		Autumn		Winter	
—	X	X	X	—	—	—	—
X	X	X	X	X	X	X	X
X	X	X	X	X	X	X	X
X	X	X	X	X	X	X	X
X	X	X	X	X	X	X	X
X	X	X	X	X	X	X	X
—	X	X	X	X	—	—	—
—	X	X	X	X	X	X	X
—	—	—	X	X	X	X	X
—	—	—	X	X	—	—	—
—	—	X	X	X	X	—	—
X	X	X	X	X	X	X	X
—	—	—	X	X	X	X	X
X	X	X	X	X	—	—	—
X	X	X	—	—	—	—	X
X	X	X	X	X	X	X	X
X	—	—	—	X	X	X	X
X	X	X	X	X	X	X	X
—	—	X	X	X	X	X	X
—	—	—	X	X	X	X	X
X	X	X	X	X	X	X	X
—	—	—	—	—	X	X	X
X	X	X	X	X	X	X	X
X	X	X	X	X	X	X	X
—	X	X	X	—	—	—	—
—	—	X	X	—	—	—	—
—	X	X	X	X	—	—	—
—	—	—	—	X	—	—	—
—	—	—	—	—	—	—	—

Key
Spring = February/March
Late spring = April/May
Summer = June/July
Late summer = August/September
Autumn = October/November
Winter = December/January

Ideally, set plants out in warm, moist soil just before or after steady rainfall.

When planting position each tree so that the best side faces the main viewpoint. If possible the stake should be on the side of the prevailing wind. The tree should be planted so that the soil mark is at the same depth as before the move.

Work in the prepared mixture, well moistened, between and around the roots. Joggle each tree up and down and firm the mixture around the roots with your heel as filling proceeds and after. If support is needed fasten the tree securely to a stake, using suitable tree ties or twine. If twine is used protect the stem or trunk with a piece of hessian or hosepipe, to prevent damage or abrasion.

Place a 50mm (2in.) layer of peat, rotted manure or compost around each tree as a mulch.

When planting on lawns, it is wise to leave a 300mm (1ft) wide collar of bare soil around the base of each conifer.

Figure 7
Planting
Left: work prepared soil in between and around the roots
Centre: firm the soil as filling proceeds
Right: each plant should be at the same depth, after planting, as previously

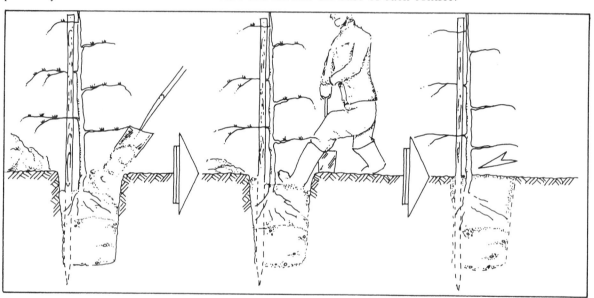

Care of conifers

Following planting the aim of the gardener should be to provide good growing conditions and to regulate growth. This involves: supplying good root conditions and a satisfactory site environment; pruning, supporting and generally caring for the conifers; and controlling pests, diseases and other problems.

Managing the soil

One of the prime needs of a young conifer is to develop and subsequently maintain a strong, healthy root system.

Water should be held by the soil, available to supply plant needs, and any surplus drained away. In dry spells water young conifers before they suffer from drought. Cover the soil around spring-planted conifers with a 50mm (2in.) minimum layer of manure, compost or peat, as a mulch to conserve moisture, and repeat this in early spring in subsequent years.

Figure 8
Aftercare
Left: leave a 300mm (1ft) collar of soil around each conifer, planted in grass
Centre: place a surface mulch around plants each spring
Right: protect newly-planted conifers from cold or drying winds

Taking care not to damage the roots, loosen the soil occasionally to prevent compaction, and enable water and air to reach the roots at lower levels.

Firm the soil around young plants loosened by wind or frost, especially in spring.

Weeds should be promptly disposed of to reduce competition for moisture, air and food. Hoe areas of bare earth during the spring and summer months, to control weeds and to conserve moisture with a surface dust mulch.

During autumn, winter or spring in the year after planting and subsequently apply 70-100g per sq. m (2–3oz. per sq. yd) of a general fertilizer, and lightly fork this in. Where growth is vigorous, reduce the dressing by half.

The feeding of old or neglected trees which are healthy, but making little growth, can often induce renewed vigour. This feeding can be done either by top dressing or by spiking and then followed by the top dressing.

Top dressing consists of spreading a 50–75mm (2–3in.) layer of soil and peat or manure mixture in the ratio of two parts soil to one part of peat or well rotted manure. Sprinkle 100g per sq.m (3oz. per sq. yd) of general fertilizer over the ground before applying the top dressing, which should cover the root area under the tree and beyond the drip line or circle – the extremities of the branches. Where peat is used, increase the amount of fertilizer by one-third.

Spiking and top dressing, when carefully carried out, can bring about an even more rapid response than top dressing alone. Make a series of holes 300mm–450mm (1–1½ft) deep, by 25–50mm (1–2in.) across, spaced 300mm (1ft) apart in the area of the feeding roots near the drip line. Fill the holes with a mixture similar to that suggested above for top dressing, or alternatively use John Innes potting compost No. 2, in either case filling the cavities right to the top.

Top dressing or spiking seems to work very well when carried out during autumn, winter or early spring before the trees break into new season's growth. However, for best results, particularly after spiking, it is more than ever important to keep the roots and soil moist during dry weather in spring and summer.

Figure 9
Feeding
Left: making holes with a crowbar, arrowed, near drip circle. Cut away section reveals cavities, arrowed
Centre inset: enlarged view of hole, filled with soil mixture
Right: broken line indicates drip circle – area of feeding roots

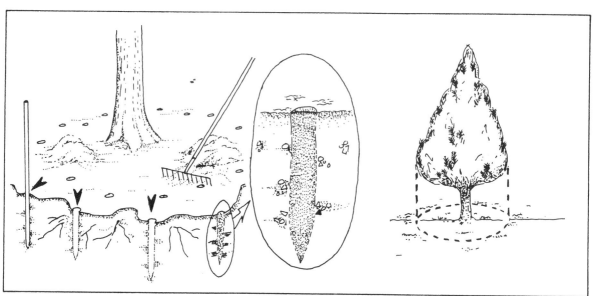

Site factors

Although there is a limit to the extent to which the environmental conditions of outdoor plants can be controlled, a moderating influence can be exerted.

Slopes which are south-facing and sunny are naturally warmest. However, cold or exposed sites can be improved by screening to give shelter from cold winds. Young conifers, and varieties with tender spring foliage in particular, can benefit greatly from the provision of even temporary wattle or hessian screens.

Coastal areas with a cool, moist climate are more favourable to the growth of some conifers than are hotter, drier and sunnier situations.

The presence of sun or shade can considerably influence the growth, habit and colouring of conifers. Many conifers, the golden and variegated forms particularly, require full sun for the strongest colouring effects. But while shade can be a limiting factor, it is tolerated by some conifers and necessary for others, especially young specimens. Some conifers, such as Tsuga, grow best in dappled shade in the early years and full sun when well established.

Give the conifers space to grow, and resist the temptation to plant them too close, which will result in overcrowding later, or at least make sure that you thin out the plants in good time.

Support and protection

One of the obvious needs of young trees is for adequate support until they become established. However, conifers planted small, 600–900mm (2–3ft) high, require very little support, often none at all and rarely anything more elaborate than a bamboo cane or stick and ties. Larger trees need more substantial support.

Large newly planted trees can be helped to resist damage from prevailing winds by guying and bracing. This method can also be used to support mature or old trees carrying heavy branches and much foliage, so long as the trees are healthy and in good condition. Hammer some strong pegs into the ground and attach the tree stems to the pegs with wires. The wires should be covered with rubber tubing or something similar (passing a wire through a length of hose pipe works well) to protect the branches from chafing. Space three, four or more straining wires evenly round the tree so that support is provided regardless of the direction of the wind.

Examine tree stakes and ties regularly and adjust or renew as necessary; stems swaying in the wind can soon be damaged.

Fastigiate conifers with ascending branches need to be gently but securely encircled with green plastic or nylon cord and tied. This prevents snow, wind and rain from disfiguring the trees.

Figure 10
Tying and supporting
Left: tree tied to prevent branches spreading under weight of snow – broken lines indicate shoots before tying
Centre: guying large tree with straining wires for support
Right: detail showing wire passed through piece of hose-pipe to protect tree

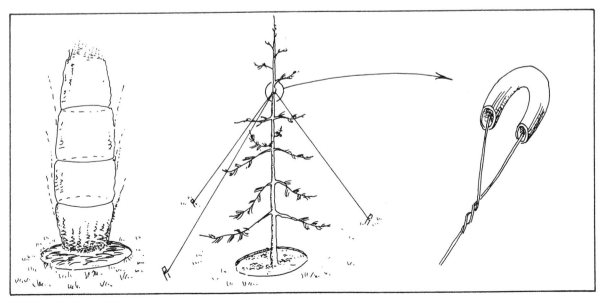

Knock snow off conifers immediately after heavy snowfalls. This is necessary to prevent breakages or trees being forced out of shape.

In country districts, especially where rabbits, hares or grey squirrels are present, protect your young conifers with plastic guards or fine mesh wire netting.

Pruning and training

This subject can be divided into four categories. The method of pruning depends to a large extent on the age and stage of a tree and its development.

Formation or training pruning consists of building up an initial framework of well spaced branches, by cutting out and removing unwanted shoots as necessary. In the case of conifers, apart from limiting the leading upright growths to one, and the regular shortening of ungainly or untidy shoots, as a rule little is needed.

The aim in training young trees is to obtain a strong main stem, which can be ensured by shortening or removing any side growths which seriously compete with the central leader for position and importance. Multi-stemmed trees, having branches with a narrow crotch (angle between branch and main stem) are less structurally sound than those with wide-angled boughs. Branches having a narrow crotch snap more easily than those with a wider angle to the main stem. As most people want quick results and suppliers are anxious to oblige, young trees can be obtained with a ready-made initial branch framework.

Normal maintenance pruning involves cutting out damaged, diseased or crossing branches and removing surplus shoots. The aim is to give branches space for proper development. With most conifers, apart from the occasional thinning, the less pruning the better.

The third category consists of what might be termed remedial pruning. Using a saw for tree surgery is sometimes necessary for safety or other reasons, or required to tidy up neglected vegetation. Difficult pruning is normally best left to qualified or professional operators. This is especially so where tree work is required at a height above that which can comfortably be reached from the top of a pair of step ladders, or where large branches are involved. However, there are jobs in this category which can be carried out by the home gardener, always provided the branch size or height involved is manageable. These are listed below.

Lopping branches: this is often necessary where trees have been neglected or are diseased. Cut back limbs to healthy wood, or flush with the main stem. Cut large branches back in sections, starting near the tips. First undercut each bough one-quarter way through close to the main stem, then cut from above, but slightly further out from the trunk. The trunk will then not be damaged by any splitting of heavy branches which may occur. The short remaining stub should be sawn off flush with the main stem. Cut or pare off any rough edges with a sharp knife, to leave a smooth finish, and paint over any wounds with lead paint or a proprietary sealant. Undercutting or root pruning: this consists of cutting around young conifers, spade deep, to sever long roots and encourage fibrous root formation. This operation is usually carried out in advance of moving or transplanting.

Figure 11
Lopping
Left: removing large limbs by
undercutting one-third way
through, and then sawing off the
limb to leave a short stump
Centre: cutting off the stump close
to the trunk
Right: paring off any rough edges
with a sharp knife before painting
the wound

Figure 12
Undercutting
Left: sever the roots spade deep
with a slanting cut, encircling the
plant, but not too close to the main
stem
Right: showing fibrous root system
a year after undercutting when
plant is ready for moving

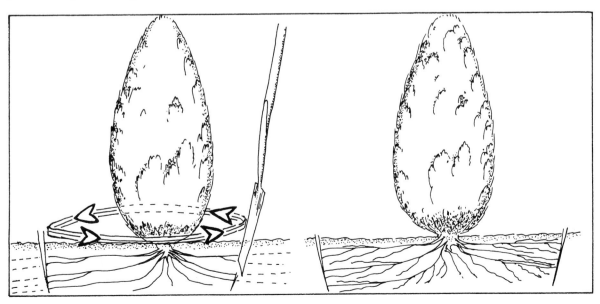

Two other pruning operations which are more generally applied to broad-leaved trees could frequently be carried out to advantage with conifers.

Crown raising: trees can sometimes be improved by the removal of some lower branches. This exposes a greater length of stem to view and leaves more space for access beneath the branches. This process can be repeated over a number of years, gradually increasing the distance betrween ground level and the lowest branches. Paint over any wounds over 25mm (1in.) in diameter left after pruning. Crown thinning: as the name suggests, this involves a reduction or cutting out of a portion of the branches in the head or crown, to let in air and daylight. This is occasionally needed, especially with neglected trees. The amount of thinning necessary varies, but the important requirement is that branches should not rub or chafe each other.

Figure 13
Pruning
Left: remove competing shoot – shown by broken line
Centre: cut out all, but one shoot-like pine shown here, below damaged leading stem. Train this shoot to replace the growing tip and tie to a temporary splint fastened to stem
Right: crown raising consists of removing the lower branches to expose the stem and give added ground clearance

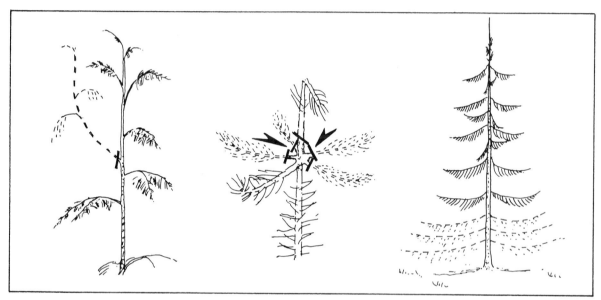

Pest and disease control
Fortunately many decorative and ornamental garden conifers escape most of these problems when given a modicum of timely attention, but they can occur from time to time. Details of the more commonly encountered pests and diseases are given in the following tables.

The most successful control measures rely heavily on preventive action against pests and diseases. Adequate space, clean cultivation, removal of dead or diseased tree parts and timely spraying where necessary will forestall most problems. With disease in particular, the application of protective or preventive sprays will not remove the blemishes. The control measures, to be successful, must start long before the symptoms occur. Leaves and shoots should be covered with a thin film of protective spray, renewed as necessary. Any badly affected parts are best cut out and burnt.

Some common conifer pests and diseases, their symptoms and control

Problem	Symptoms	Control
Pests		
Adelges	White 'wool' patches and yellowing needles, or, on shoots of Spruce, pineapple-like galls. Host plants also include Larch and Pine.	Spray affected conifers with HCH preparations and give a repeat spray in spring as a preventive measure.
Aphids	Colonies of blue or green insects near growing points leaving honeydew, a sticky shiny deposit, on leaves and stems. Occur mainly on Spruce.	Spray affected conifers with derris, dimethoate or malathion.
Beetles and weevils	Sickly and dying young conifers with the bark eaten at or near ground level, or yellowing shoots with bark or rind removed. Most conifers can be affected.	Spray or dust young conifer stems in spring with HCH as preventive. Spray affected larger plants and repeat each spring.
Cockchafer	Sickly or dying seedling conifers with eaten roots; fleshy white larvae with brown heads in the soil near affected plants. Many conifer species can be attacked.	Difficult to control, but clean cultivation, adequate pre-planting preparation and weed control are useful preventive measures.
Conifer spinning mites	Sickly greyish or yellow-brown foliage with reddish orange eggs and mites appearing in spring among fine webbing. Host plants include Juniper, Spruce and Thuja.	Spray with malathion in spring, giving a repeat spray after 14–21 days.
Juniper webber moth caterpillars	Juniper foliage bound together with webbing and dead leaves; colonies of small brownish caterpillars.	Apply two or three sprays of HCH at 14–21 day intervals. Alternatively use fenitrothion.
Pine looper caterpillars	Needles of Pine devoured by greenish caterpillars with white or cream longitudinal stripes.	Apply fenitrothion spray and repeat 14 days later.
Pine shoot moth caterpillars	Small white or greenish yellow grubs which bore into young shoots, of Pine and Larch mainly. Firs may also be attacked, however.	Very difficult to control once inside the shoots. As a preventive apply HCH sprays or dusts in spring. Alternatively use fenitrothion.
Red spider mites	Pale needles or foliage with numerous small reddish or yellow insects on fine webbing among the foliage. Spruce and other conifers are affected.	Apply two or three sprays of derris, dimethoate or malathion at 14–21 day intervals in spring or summer.

Scale (various)	Brownish or dirty whitish scales on shoots or stems accompanied by poor growth. Junipers are often affected.	Give two or three sprays of diazinon or malathion at 10–14 day intervals.

Diseases

Botrytis or grey mould	Grey mould on needles and foliage, causing dieback in severe cases. Most conifers can be attacked, especially Firs, Spruce, Hemlock, Cupressus and Sequoia.	Improve air circulation, remove affected foliage and spray with benomyl.
Canker	Firs develop witches' brooms, a mass of shoots at affected areas, causing cankers and sometimes death.	Cut out affected branches and avoid overcrowding.
Conifer heart rot	Young trees dead or dying, old trees stunted, with soft or slimy heart wood which turns pink. Most conifers can be affected.	Remove affected trees and improve growing conditions, correcting excessively wet or very dry conditions.
Damping off	Germinating and young seedlings collapsing and dying. Most seed-raised conifers can be affected.	As preventive measures dress seed with thiram and water with captan before sowing.
Dieback	See Botrytis.	
Honey fungus (Armillaria)	Honey-coloured toadstools on dead trees and bushes at ground level; black boot-lace-like thongs or polymorphs in the soil near the affected plant. Kills young woody plants including conifers and broad-leafed trees and shrubs.	Dig out and burn affected plants and polymorphs. Sterilize the ground with a 2 per cent solution of formaldehyde and allow 4–6 weeks for the fumes to disperse before planting.
Leaf cast	Brown, black or white small spots, depending on the causal organism, occurring on leaf undersides. The needles turn brownish, fall off and die. Wet, dull seasons favour leaf cast disease. Most conifers can be affected.	Apply copper based fungicide sprays and repeat each spring.
Pine rust	Bright yellow dust on leaves and shoots of Pine. This rust can also affect Aspen Poplars. Scots Pine is the main conifer affected.	Avoid planting Scots Pine or its varieties near Aspen Poplars. Allow Pines space to develop and encourage good air circulation.
Thuja leaf blight	Browning and toppling over of seedlings, sometimes killing them. Thuja is the main conifer affected.	Apply copper-based fungicide spray, remove infected foliage and mulch trees to encourage new growth.

Sprays should not be made up indoors and should be thoroughly mixed before use.
Spraying or dusting should not be carried out in wet, freezing or windy conditions.

Propagation

Conifers can be increased by seeds, cuttings, layering and grafting. All of these methods except grafting can be carried out with few if any real problems by enthusiastic gardeners. The chief requirements are patience and attention to detail. Seeds can take up to a year and a half or more to germinate, and anything from a further one to three years before seedlings can be safely planted out. Cuttings, likewise, can take up to two years to root and may need a growing-on period of one to three years after that. Layering can be slightly quicker, saving perhaps one or two years.

The methods of increase to use for specific conifers are given in the second part of this book.

Raising from seed

Small quantities of seed are best sown thinly in boxes or pots containing John Innes seed compost or an equivalent mixture.

Most conifer seeds are sown when fresh, but seeds of some Firs are best stratified before sowing. Stratification consists of mixing seeds with sand and subjecting them to winter frost and cold, outside, but well protected from birds and vermin. The effect of frost and moisture is to speed up the rate of germination when seeds are sown in spring.

Unheated frame will usually provide the correct conditions for germinating seeds. Seeds must be protected from strong sun, and seedlings should be lightly shaded from strong sunlight during the first growing season.

There is always the possibility that among your seedlings a new form or variant may arise.

Vegetative reproduction

CUTTINGS

Cuttings provide a useful method of increase for many conifers. Easy kinds such as chamaecyparis can be rooted in nothing more elaborate than a cold frame. Varieties from the following genera can usually be raised from cuttings without undue difficulties: Chamaecyparis; Cryptomeria; x Cupressocyparis; Juniperus; Taxus; and Thuja. Cuttings from Cedrus, Pinus and Pseudotsuga can present problems.

Cuttings of one or two-year-old wood are taken from the parent plant with a heel attached, usually during late summer. A 'heel' cutting consists of a shoot 50–150mm (2–6in.) long with a piece of older stem attached at the point of severage. The heel should be trimmed with a sharp knife, removing any straggly ends, and then dipped in a hormone rooting preparation. Insert the prepared cuttings to one-third to half their length around the edge of 75–100mm (3–4in.) pots or suitable containers, filled with cutting compost. A mixture consisting of equal parts of sand and peat is excellent.Keep the cuttings moist, shaded from strong sun and protected from frost. Rooted cuttings may be planted out in spring in a lightly shaded position

LAYERING

This is usually best done in autumn. Cut long two-year-old growths obliquely two-thirds through 100–150mm (4–6in.) from the tip. Some successful gardeners remove two slithers of rind about 25mm (1in.)

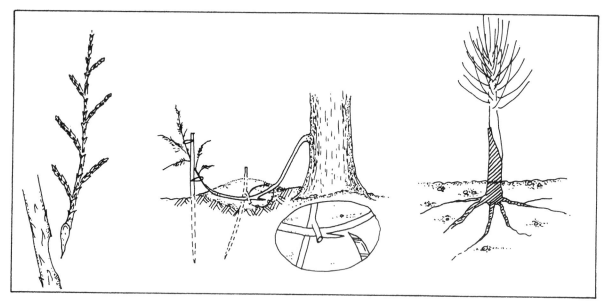

Figure 14
Propagation
Left: heel cutting, with piece of older stem attached before trimming
Centre: layering, showing piece of stem with slanting cut, pegged down in hollow, filled with prepared soil
Right: an established graft union of rootstock (hatched) and scion or shoot. Grafting is often used to increase conifers.

long, instead of cutting the stem. Peg them down into hollows and cover with prepared compost. These layers can be severed from the parent plant when they have rooted, which may be 12–24 months later. They may then be planted out.

GRAFTING
This method is used for choice varieties of conifers which do not breed true from seed, or need the roots of another but closely related variety for best results. Grafting is very specialized and is usually left to the professional.

The conifers

Choosing a conifer

Before going into the detailed descriptions of each conifer, readers may like to consult the following lists, which have been compiled for quick and easy reference.

Conifers for alkaline or chalk soils
Abies pinsapo
Cedrus atlantica
Cephalotaxus harringtonia
Chamaecyparis lawsoniana
Chamaecyparis nootkatensis
x Cupressocyparis leylandii
Ginkgo biloba
Juniperus chinensis
Juniperus communis
Juniperus x media
Juniperus recurva
Juniperus sabina
Juniperus virginiana
Picea omorika
Pinus mugo
Pinus nigra
Pinus sylvestris
Taxus baccata
Thuja occidentalis
Thuja orientalis
Thuja plicata

Conifers for acid soils
Abies balsamea
Abies concolor
Abies delavayi forrestii
Abies koreana
Abies lasiocarpa
Chamaecyparis nootkatensis
Chamaecyparis obtusa
Chamaecyparis pisifera
Chamaecyparis thyoides
Cryptomeria japonica
Cupressus glabra
Ginkgo biloba
Juniperus horizontalis
Juniperus scopulorum
Juniperus squamata
Picea abies
Picea breweriana
Picea glauca
Picea omorika
Picea orientalis
Picea pungens
Pinus aristata
Pinus cembra
Pinus heldreichi leucodermis
Pinus mugo
Pinus parviflora

Pseudotsuga menziesii
Thuja occidentalis
Thuja orientalis

Conifers for cold sites
Chamaecyparis lawsoniana
Chamaecyparis nootkatensis
x Cupressocyparis leylandii
Juniperus communis
Juniperus horizontalis
Picea abies
Picea glauca
Picea omorika
Pinus mugo
Pinus sylvestris
Pseudotsuga menziesii
Taxus baccata

Conifers for shaded sites (buildings and north-facing slopes)
Abies balsamea
Abies delavayi forrestii
Abies lasiocarpa
Cephalotaxus harringtonia
Chamaecyparis lawsoniana
Chamaecyparis nootkatensis
Chamaecyparis pisifera
Chemaecyparis thyoides
Cryptomeria japonica
x Cupressocyparis leylandii
Juniperus conferta
Juniperus x media
Juniperus recurva
Picea abies
Picea breweriana
Picea glauca
Picea omorika
Picea orientalis
Pinus sylvestris
Pseudotsuga menziesii
Taxus baccata

Conifers for coastal districts
Provided the requirements of soil, shade, and shelter are met, all conifers can be satisfactorily grown in coastal districts. Varieties particularly well suited include the following.
Abies pinsapo
Abies pinsapo 'Glauca'

Cedrus deodara
Chamaecyparis lawsoniana and varieties
Chamaecyparis pisifera and varieties
Chamaecyparis thyoides
x Cupressocyparis leylandii and varieties
Juniperus communis and varieties
Juniperus conferta
Juniperus x media and varieties
Juniperus sabina and varieties
Pinus cembra and varieties
Pinus mugo and varieties
Pinus nigra and varieties
Pinus parviflora
Pinus sylvestris and varieties
Taxus baccata and varieties
Thuja plicata

Conifers for town planting
Abies balsamea 'Hudsonia'
Abies koreana
Abies koreana 'Compact Dwarf'
Calocedrus decurrens
Cephalotaxus harringtonia
Cephalotaxus harringtonia drupacea
Chamaecyparis lawsoniana and varieties
Chamaecyparis thyoides and varieties
x Cupressocyparis leylandii and varieties
Ginkgo biloba
Juniperus communis and varieties
Juniperus x media and varieties
Juniperus virginiana and varieties
Picea omorika and varieties
Pinus aristata
Pinus mugo 'Gnom'
Pinus mugo pumilio
Pinus sylvestris 'Beuvronensis'
Pinus sylvelstris 'Pygmaea'
Pinus sylvestris 'Watereri'
Taxodium distichum
Taxodium distichum 'Pendens'
Taxus baccata and varieties
Thuja plicata and varieties

Pyramidal conifers
The majority of conifers conform

to a pyramidal or conical habit of growth. The width, relative to height, varies with age, being usually narrower in young plants and broadening with age.

Abies balsamea
Abies concolor
Abies concolor 'Glauca Compacta'
Abies delavayi
Abies koreana
Abies koreana 'Compact Dwarf'
Abies lasiocarpa
Abies lasiocarpa arizonica
Abies lasiocarpa 'Compacta'
Abies pinsapo
Abies pinsapo 'Aurea'
Abies pinsapo 'Glauca'
Calocedrus decurrens 'Aureovariegata'
Cedrus atlantica 'Aurea'
Cedrus deodara 'Aurea'
Cedrus deodara 'Verticillata Glauca'
Chamaecyparis lawsoniana
Chamaecyparis lawsoniana 'Allumii'
Chamaecyparis lawsoniana 'Erecta'
Chamaecyparis lawsoniana 'Erecta Aurea'
Chamaecyparis lawsoniana 'Lanei'
Chamaecyparis lawsoniana 'Lutea'
Chamaecyparis lawsoniana 'Stewartii'
Chamaecyparis lawsoniana Wisselii'
Chamaecyparis nootkatensis
Chamaecyparis nootkatensis 'Glauca'
Chamaecyparis nootkatensis 'Lutea'
Chamaecyparis obtusa 'Crippsii'
Chamaecyparis pisifera
Chamaecyparis pisifera 'Boulevard'
Chamaecyparis thyoides
Chamaecyparis thyoides 'Ericoides'
Chamaecyparis thyoides 'Glauca'
Cryptomeria japonica
Cryptomeria japonica 'Elegans'
x Cupressocyparis leylandii 'Castlewellan Gold'
x Cupressocyparis leylandii 'Green Spire'
x Cupressocyparis leylandii 'Naylor's Blue'
Cupressus glabra
Cupressus glabra 'Aurea'

Fastigiate conifers
Calocedrus decurrens
Juniperus communis 'Hibernica'
Juniperus scopulorum 'Blue Heaven'
Juniperus virginiana 'Skyrocket'

Narrow columnar conifers
Abies balsamea
Abies concolor
Calocedrus decurrens

Chamaecyparis lawsoniana 'Columnaris'
Chamaecyparis lawsoniana 'Ellwoodii'
Chamaecyparis lawsoniana 'Ellwood's Gold'
Chamaecyparis lawsoniana 'Erecta'
Chamaecyparis lawsoniana 'Erecta Aurea'
Chamaecyparis lawsoniana 'Lutea'
Chamaecyparis lawsoniana 'Pottenii'
Chamaecyparis nootkatensis
Chamaecyparis obtusa
Chamaecyparis thyoides 'Andelyensis'
Cupressus glabra 'Pyramidalis'
Juniperus chinensis
Juniperus chinensis 'Aurea'
Juniperus chinensis 'Pyramidalis'
Juniperus communis 'Compressa'
Juniperus communis 'Hibernica'
Juniperus scopulorum 'Springbank'
Juniperus virginiana 'Skyrocket'
Picea omorika
Taxodium distichum
Taxus baccata 'Fastigiata'
Taxus baccata 'Fastigiata Aurea'

Broad upright conifers
Chamaecyparis lawsoniana 'Ellwoodii'
Chamaecyparis lawsoniana 'Ellwood's Gold'
Chamaecyparis lawsoniana 'Pottenii'
Ginkgo biloba 'Fastigiata'
Juniperus chinensis
Juniperus chinensis 'Aurea'
Juniperus communis 'Compressa'
Taxus baccata 'Fastigiata'
Taxus baccata 'Fastigiata Aurea'
Thuja orientalis 'Elegantissima'

Globose or rounded conifers
Abies balsamea 'Hudsonia'
Cedrus libani 'Nana'
Cephalotaxus harringtonia
Cephalotaxus harringtonia drupacea
Chamaecyparis lawsoniana 'Minima Aurea'
Chamaecyparis lawsoniana 'Minima Glauca'
Chamaecyparis nootkatensis 'Compacta'
Chamaecyparis obtusa 'Nana'
Chamaecyparis obtusa 'Nana Aurea'
Chamaecyparis obtusa 'Nana Gracilis'
Chamaecyparis obtusa 'Pygmaea'
Chamaecyparis pisifera 'Nana'
Cryptomeria japonica 'Globosa Nana'
Cryptomeria japonica 'Lobbii Nana'

Cryptomeria japonica 'Vilmoriniana'
Juniperus squamata 'Blue Star'
Juniperus squamata 'Meyeri'
Picea abies 'Clanbrassilliana'
Picea abies 'Nidiformis'
Pinus mugo 'Gnom'
Pinus mugo pumilio
Pinus sylvestris 'Beuvronensis'
Pseudotsuga menziesii 'Fletcheri'
Thuja occidentalis 'Lutea Nana'
Thuja orientalis 'Rosedalis'

Weeping (pendulous) conifers
Cedrus atlantica 'Glauca Pendula'
Cedrus deodara 'Aurea Pendula'
Cedrus deodara 'Pendula'
Chamaecyparis nootkatensis 'Pendula'
Ginkgo biloba 'Pendula'
Juniperus recurva coxii
Picea breweriana
Picea omorika 'Pendula'
Picea orientalis 'Pendula'

Spreading tree forms
Many kinds of conifer, including several species and varieties of Abies, Cedrus, Picea and Pinus, become spreading and flat-topped with age. The more notable species include the following.
Abies lasiocarpa
Abies pinsapo
Cedrus atlantica
Cedrus atlantica glauca
Cedrus deodara
Cedrus libani
Juniperus x media
Picea abies
Picea pungens
Pinus nigra
Pinus sylvestris

Spreading shrub forms
Chamaecyparis obtusa 'Tetragona Aurea'
Chamaecyparis pisifera 'Filifera'
Chamaecyparis pisifera 'Filifera Aurea'
Cryptomeria japonica 'Lobbii Nana'
Juniperus x media 'Blaauw'
Juniperus x media 'Hetzii'
Juniperus x media 'Old Gold'
Juniperus x media 'Pfitzerana Aurea'
Juniperus sabina 'Arcadia'
Juniperus sabina 'Blue Danube'

Procumbent or prostrate conifers
Juniperus communis 'Depressa Aurea'
Juniperus communis 'Repanda'
Juniperus conferta
Juniperus horizontalis

Juniperus horizontalis 'Glauca'
Juniperus horizontalis 'Montana'
Juniperus horizontalis 'Wiltonii'
Juniperus procumbens
Juniperus procumbens 'Nana'
Juniperus recurva 'Embley Park'
Juniperus sabina 'Skandia'
Juniperus sabina 'Tamariscifolia'

Procumbent ground-cover conifers
Juniperus communis 'Depressa
    Aurea'
Juniperus communis 'Repanda'
Juniperus conferta
Juniperus horizontalis
Juniperus horizontalis 'Douglasii'
Juniperus horizontalis 'Glauca'
Juniperus horizontalis 'Montana'
Juniperus horizontalis 'Plumosa'
Juniperus horizontalis 'Wiltonii'
Juniperus procumbens
Juniperus procumbens 'Nana'
Juniperus recurva 'Embley Park'
Juniperus sabina 'Arcadia'
Juniperus sabina 'Tamariscifolia'
Picea abies 'Nidiformis'
Picea abies Procumbens'
Picea pungens 'Globosa'
Taxus baccata 'Repandens'

Dwarf conifers
Abies balsamea 'Hudsonia'
Abies concolor 'Glauca Compacta'
Abies koreana 'Compact Dwarf'
Abies lasiocarpa 'Compacta'
Cedrus libani 'Nana'
Chamaecyparis lawsoniana 'Minima
    Aurea'
Chamaecyparis lawsoniana 'Minima
    Glauca'
Chamaecyparis obtusa 'Nana'
Chamaecyparis obtusa 'Nana Aurea'
Chamaecyparis obtusa 'Nana
    Gracilis'
Chamaecyparis obtusa 'Pygmaea'
Chamaecyparis pisifera 'Nana'
Chamaecyparis thyoides 'Ericoides'
Cryptomeria japonica 'Globosa
    Nana'
Cryptomeria japonica 'Lobbii Nana'
Cryptomeria japonica 'Vilmoriniana'
Juniperus chinensis 'Japonica'
Juniperus communis 'Compressa'
Juniperus communis 'Depressa
    Aurea'
Juniperus squamata 'Blue Star'
Picea abies 'Pumila'
Picea glauca albertiana 'Conica'
Picea pungens 'Globosa'
Pinus mugo 'Gnom'
Pinus nigra 'Hornibrookiana'
Pinus sylvestris 'Beuvronensis'
Pseudotsuga menziesii 'Fletcheri'

Taxus baccata 'Adpressa Variegata'
Thuja occidentalis 'Hetz' Midget'
Thuja occidentalis 'Rheingold'
Thuja orientalis 'Aurea Nana'
Thuja orientalis 'Rosedalis'
Thuja plicata 'Rogersii'
Thuja plicata 'Stoneham Gold'

Yellow or gold conifers
Abies pinsapo 'Aurea'
Calocedrus decurrens
    'Aureovariegata'
Cedrus atlantica 'Aurea'
Cedrus deodara 'Aurea'
Cedrus deodara 'Aurea Pendula'
Chamaecyparis lawsoniana
    'Ellwood's Gold'
Chamaecyparis lawsoniana 'Erecta
    Aurea'
Chamaecyparis lawsoniana 'Lanei'
Chamaecyparis lawsoniana 'Lutea'
Chamaecyparis lawsoniana 'Minima
    Aurea'
Chamaecyparis lawsoniana
    'Stewartii'
Chamaecyparis nootkatensis
    'Lutea'
Chamaecyparis obtusa 'Crippsii'
Chamaecyparis obtusa 'Nana Aurea'
Chamaecyparis obtusa 'Nana Lutea'
Chamaecyparis obtusa 'Tetragona
    Aurea'
Chamaecyparis pisifera 'Filifera
    Aurea'
Chamaecyparis pisifera 'Squarrosa
    Sulphurea'
Juniperus chinensis 'Aurea'
Juniperus communis 'Depressa
    Aurea'
Juniperus x media 'Old Gold'
Juniperus x media 'Pfitzerana Aurea'
Juniperus x media 'Plumosa Aurea'
Picea orientalis 'Aurea'
Pinus cembra 'Aureovariegata'
Pinus sylvestris 'Aurea'
Taxus baccata 'Adpressa Variegata'
Taxus baccata 'Fastigiata
    Aureomarginata'
Taxus baccata 'Semperaurea'
Thuja occidentalis 'Aurea'
Thuja occidentalis 'Lutea Nana'
Thuja occidentalis 'Rheingold'
Thuja orientalis 'Aurea Nana'
Thuja orientalis 'Elegantissima'
Thuja plicata 'Rogersii'
Thuja plicata 'Stoneham Gold'
Thuja plicata 'Zebrina'

Blue conifers
Abies concolor 'Glauca Compacta'
Abies pinsapo 'Glauca'
Cedrus atlantica glauca
Cedrus atlantica 'Glauca Pendula'
Chamaecyparis lawsoniana 'Allumii'

Chamaecyparis lawsoniana
    'Columnaris'
Chamaecyparis pisifera 'Boulevard'
Cupressus glabra
Cupressus glabra 'Pyramidalis'
Juniperus chinensis
    The following two as young
plants.
Juniperus chinensis 'Japonica'
Juniperus chinensis 'Pyramidalis'
Juniperus horizontalis 'Glauca'
Juniperus scopulorum
Juniperus scopulorum 'Blue Heaven'
Juniperus scopulorum 'Springbank'
Juniperus squamata 'Blue Star'
Juniperus squamata 'Meyeri'
Juniperus virginiana
Juniperus virginiana 'Burkii'
Juniperus virginiana 'Cupressifolia'
Juniperus virginiana 'Glauca'
Picea abies
Picea abies 'Acrocona'
Picea glauca
Picea glauca albertiana 'Conica'
Picea omorika
Picea orientalis
Picea orientalis 'Aurea'
Picea pungens
Picea pungens 'Endtz'
Picea pungens glauca
Picea pungens 'Globosa'
Picea pungens 'Koster'
Picea pungens 'Moerheimii'
Pinus aristata
Pinus cembra
Pinus cembra 'Jermyns'
Pinus heldreichi leucodermis
Pinus nigra 'Hornibrookiana'
Pinus nigra maritima
Pinus parviflora 'Adcock's Dwarf'
Pinus parviflora 'Brevifolia'
Pinus parviflora 'Glauca'
Pinus sylvestris 'Aurea'
Pinus sylvestris 'Watereri' as a young
    plant
Taxodium distichum
Taxodium distichum 'Pendens'
Thuja occidentalis as a young plant
Thuja occidentalis 'Aurea'
Thuja occidentalis 'Holmstrupii'
Thuja occidentalis 'Rheingold'
Thuja orientalis
Thuja plicata
Thuja plicata 'Stoneham Gold'
Thuja plicata 'Zebrina'

Explanatory notes to individual descriptions of conifers

The information about each conifer is necessarily brief and some qualifications of the comments are essential to enable the reader to grasp the facts easily.

The conifer named at the start of each table is the type or species, which in many cases has given rise to one or more varieties. The outline of uses, description, requirements and notes on culture relate to the species except where otherwise stated.

Names The name given consisting of two words is the species or botanical name currently in use, followed by the family of plants e.g. (botanical) *Abies balsamea* (family) Pinaceae. The subsequent names are the English or American popular equivalents.

Uses Differences of size, habit or colour mean that most conifers are better suited to some purposes than to others.

Description The appearance, dimensions, growth rate and life span are influenced greatly by local conditions of climate, site, soil and method of cultivation. The facts and figures given are approximate and represent average characteristics likely to be encountered under normal garden conditions. However, considerable variation can and does occur.

Features The comments on the main qualities which make a tree attractive relate to the species unless indicated otherwise.

Pollution In towns and cities, fumes and gases in the air, soot, oil and other deposits are a normal hazard to plants. Those conifers which can grow and flourish in spite of these difficulties are indicated as being tolerant or resistant.

Non-poisonous trees are those which normally present no danger to people or pets.

Varieties When conifers are being chosen for a particular purpose or characteristic, often a variety will be found to be more suitable than the species from which it originated. While a conifer type, for example, may be suitable only for large spaces, dwarf varieties, appropriate for confined areas, are often available.

Requirements The growth and development of garden trees depends largely on how well or otherwise their needs are satisfied with regard to climate, site, soil and other influences. Where conditions are less than perfect, growth and development will also fall short of the best results possible. An indication of the ideal conditions (which are often difficult to provide) is given, together with the degree of latitude that is possible. Of course, seasonal and weather variations can upset the best calculations, even when other requirements are met.

Notes on culture

Planting Generally small conifers can be transplanted more easily and will become established more readily in new surroundings than large specimens, often quickly catching up and overtaking the latter. The season of planting and suggested size refer to lifted open-ground trees except where stated to the contrary.

Space The area or distance indicated is the space needed by average conifers at maturity.

Pruning   Requirements here vary according to the size and stage of development of individual trees.

Plant associations   Some indication is given of plants which have been found to associate well. Gardeners will of course wish to try their own combinations too. Dwarf conifers and heathers are usually attractive when planted together, for example.

Pest and disease control   These notes should be read in conjuction with the table on pages 29–30.

Propagation   The methods indicated are those most usually adopted. The propagation of conifers is a time-consuming excercise, and most people prefer to buy young conifers rather than try to raise them. However, an understanding of how conifers are raised can be helpful in their planting and aftercare. For example, to avoid scion-rooting it is important not to plant grafted conifers too deeply.

Season of interest table   This is designed to indicate the main features and the approximate time they can be seen and enjoyed. Items are self-explanatory. Where an entry is omitted, the feature concerned is either insignificant or lacking.

Growth rate and qualities table   The dimensions given are examples of the average rate of growth which can be expected under normal garden conditions. Differences in planting size will be reflected in the height and width at five and at twenty years.

The root spread   at planting time will usually approximate to the width in the case of open-ground trees. With container-grown plants the spread of roots can vary from one-third to two-thirds the width above ground.

Hardiness   in plants is the ability to survive without special protection in normal conditions. This quality is dependent to a very large extent on climate, and on local factors such as altitude, aspect, exposure and cultivation. For our purposes here the conifers have been classified according to hardiness into three main categories, A, B and C, which relate to the climatic zones on the maps on pages 13–14. Trees in category:

A can be grown in a cool temperate zone
B can be grown in a mild temperate zone
C can be grown in a warm temperate zone

Plants which are borderline are indicated by two letters, that is, A/B or B/C. Of course, in any broad climatic zone there are areas which are particularly favourable or otherwise. Locations that are at high altitudes, or are exposed or north-facing, in, say, climatic zone B, for example, might provide conditions equivalent to zone A.

Wind-firm

1 = very secure rooting
2 = normally wind-firm
3 = only moderately wind-firm – which may mean staking for many years in exposed situations.

Plant care profile   Minimum, average and high refer to the degree of attention that is normally required to keep trees healthy, tidy and in good condition.

Maintenance covers such aspects as pest and disease control, leaf clearance, feeding and other cultural requirements.

Abies balsamea – PINACEAE

Balsam Fir

A hardy evergreen tree.
Origin   North-eastern USA.

Uses
The true Balsam Fir is not now widely planted in gardens, but the Dwarf Balsam Fir is an excellent plant for rock gardens.

Description
Dimensions   Ultimate size rarely exceeds 7.5–9m (25–30ft) high by 2–3m (7–10ft) wide.
Rate of growth   Moderate to slow.
Life span   Variable, but usually fairly short, up to 45 years.
Habit   Usually pyramidal, broadening with age.
Leaves   A glossy mid-green on the upper surface in spring, fading in autumn. The winter buds are round, red and resinous.
Flowers   Insignificant.
Fruits   Purple or olive green cones, borne by mature trees.
Bark   Inconspicuous.

Features
This Fir produces a transparent resin known as Canadian Balsam, which has earned it the popular name of Balsam Fir. The type, unlike its dwarf variety, is not particularly reliable as a garden conifer, tending to become untidy after a few years. Hardy and windfirm.
Pollution   Fairly tolerant.
Non-poisonous.

Variety
Abies balsamea 'Hudsonia' (Dwarf Balsam Fir). The principal variety of note, a dwarf conifer of rounded habit, rarely exceeding 600–750mm (2–2½ft) high by 600–900mm (2–3ft) wide. A very hardy conifer, it is slow-growing and has shiny green leaves.

Requirements
Position   A mild temperate climate suits these conifers, and, especially when young, they need a lightly shaded situation protected from late spring frosts. Moist air conditions, as on valley sides in lowland areas of moist or humid districts, suit them better than dry conditions.

Soil   Almost any well drained, but moist loam is adequate for young plants. Deeper, moist loams that are slightly acid, pH 6–6.5, are nearer the ideal for mature trees.

Notes on culture
Planting   Plant small conifers, up to 300mm (1ft) high, in autumn or late spring. Staking and tying is not necessary for the dwarf variety or small plants, but larger trees need support until firmly rooted. Keep the ground around young plants weed-free.
Space   Allow the Balsam Fir a minimum area of 4.5m (15ft) diameter at maturity, and avoid planting closer to buildings than 7.5m (25ft). The Dwarf Balsam Fir needs only 900mm (3ft) diameter.
Pruning   Prune *A. balsamea* to limit main shoots to one central leader, and cut back any damaged, diseased or untidy shoots to maintain a good shape. It is neither necessary nor desirable to limit *A. b.* 'Hudsonia' to one central stem, but trimming to shape can usefully be carried out. All pruning should be done in late spring.

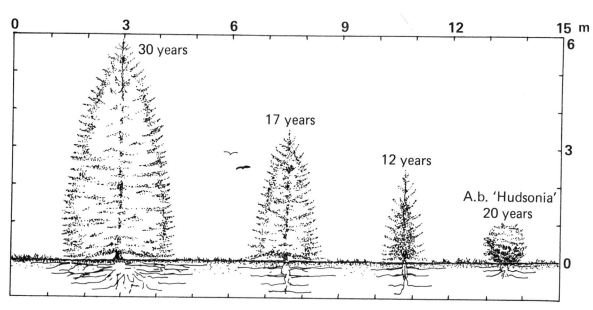

30 years

17 years

12 years

A.b. 'Hudsonia'
20 years

Plant associations The Dwarf Balsam Fir makes a pleasing combination with heathers.

Pest and disease control Adelges, which weaken plants by feeding on them, under waxy, wool-like, whitish tufts on branches, can be controlled by HCH sprays as necessary. To check dieback of branches, caused by fungus diseases, remove affected parts and train or encourage new shoots to fill any gaps. Rusts, which occur as white pustules on leaves, may be caused by any one of several fungi. To control, avoid overcrowding, and in severe cases spray with a copper or thiram fungicide.

Propagation By seed sown in spring. Named varieties by layering in autumn or grafting in spring.

Season of interest	Winter	Spring	Late spring	Summer	Late summer	Autumn
In full leaf	X—	———	———	———	———	—X
Autumn colour						
Flowers						
Fruits				X—	———	—X
Bark and stem	—	—X			X—	—

The following five characteristics determine to a great extent the amount of attention a specific tree requires.

	When planted	5 years	20 years
Height	300 mm	1·0 m	3·0 - 5·0 m
Width	100 mm	300 mm	1·0 - 2·5 m
Root spread	100 mm	400 mm	2·5 - 3·0 m
Hardiness	C	B	B
Wind-firm	3	2	1

Plant care profile

	Minimum	Average	High
Site needs		X——	——X
Soil needs		X	
Pruning	X		
Staking	X		
Maintenance	X——	——X	

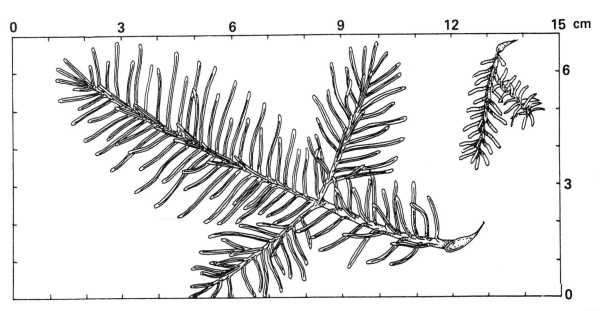

Abies concolor – PINACEAE
Colorado White Fir

A hardy evergreen tree.
Origin   Western USA and Mexico.

Uses
The Colorado White Fir and its
varieties make excellent specimens
when planted on their own in grass
or on lawns, The variety *A.c.*
'Glauca Compacta' can be used in
small gardens or among rocks.

Description
Dimensions   Average ultimate size
10–15m (33–50ft) high by 3–4.5m
(10–15ft) wide.
Rate of growth   Slow to rapid,
rather variable depending on soil
and climate.
Life span   This Fir can reasonably
be expected to live 60 years or
more.
Habit   Symmetrical and pyramidal.
The branches are arranged in
whorls, radiating from the main
trunk.
Leaves   Grey-green, usually almost
vertical from the shoots.
Flowers   Insignificant.
Fruits   Cones which are green and
purple at first, turning brownish
when ripe.
Bark   Smooth, often resin-blistered.

Features
The Colorado Fir and its varieties
are among the most attractive of
conifers. They do not appear to
have any serious faults.
Pollution   Moderately tolerant.
Non-poisonous.

Varieties
Abies concolor 'Glauca Compacta'.
A small tree of bushy habit,
growing to approximately 2.5m
(8ft) high by about the same wide.
Produces very glaucous grey-blue
new foliage in early summer.
Abies concolor 'Violacea'. One of
the best of the glaucous forms.
Abies concolor 'Wattezii'. New
foliage an attractive silvery yellow.

Requirements
Position   A sunny but sheltered
situation in an area with a mild
temperate climate suits these trees.
Sites exposed to cold north and
east winds should be avoided.
Soil   A deep, well drained but
moist loam, well supplied with
humus. and acid to neutral, pH
6–7, is near the ideal.

Notes on culture
Planting   Plant small conifers,
about 300mm (1ft) high, in autumn
or late spring. Staking and tying is
not necessary for small plants, but
larger ones need support until
firmly rooted.
Space   Allow a minimum area of
5m (17ft) diameter at maturity, and
to prevent excessive shade to house
windows avoid planting closer to
dwellings than 9m (30ft). In the
case of the variety *A.c.* 'Glauca
Compacta' the diameter may be
reduced to 2.5m (8ft).
Pruning   Prune tree forms to limit
main shoots to one central leader.
On all types cut back any damaged,
diseased or untidy shoots to
maintain a good shape. All pruning
should be done in spring.
Plant associations   This fir is
effective when contrasted with red
or crimson leaved kinds of berberis
and prunus.
A.c. 'Glauca Compacta' looks well
when planted among other dwarf
conifers, or with heathers or rock
plants.

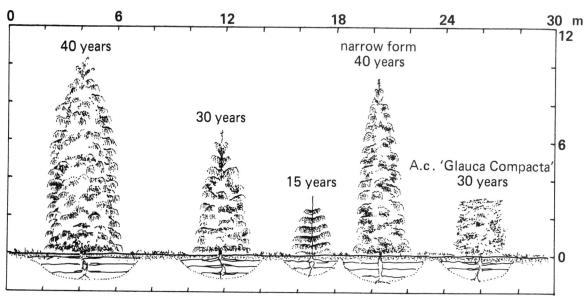

Pest and disease control Adelges, apparent by waxy white tufts on branches, can be controlled by HCH sprays. Aphids, which occasionally attack shoot tips, can be controlled by malathion sprays. Dieback is best kept in check by cutting out any dead or dying shoots. Rusts, causing white pustules on leaves, are not usually serious in gardens: to control, avoid overcrowding, and if necessary spray with a copper or thiram fungicide.

Propagation By seed sown in spring. Named varieties by grafting in spring.

Season of interest	Winter	Spring	Late spring	Summer	Late summer	Autumn
In full leaf	X—					—X
Autumn colour						
Flowers						
Fruits				X—		—X
Bark and stem	—X				X—	

The following five characteristics determine to a great extent the amount of attention a specific tree requires.

	When planted	5 years	20 years
Height	300 mm	2·0 m	5·0 – 7·0 m
Width	100 mm	600mm	2·5 m
Root spread	100 mm	1·0 m	3·5 m
Hardiness	C	B	B
Wind-firm	3	2	1

Plant care profile

	Minimum	Average	High
Site needs		X	
Soil needs		X	
Pruning		X	
Staking	X		
Maintenance	X———	X	

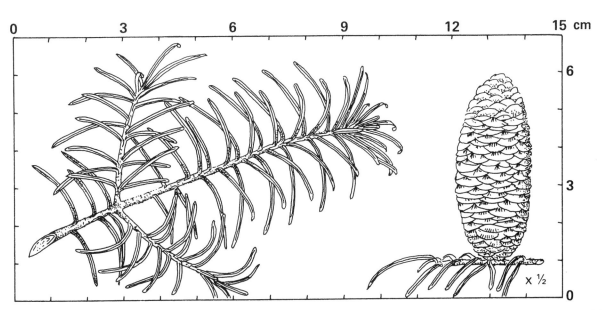

x ½

41

Abies delavayi forrestii – PINACEAE
Forrest's Fir, Silver Fir

A moderately hardy evergreen tree.
Origin   South-western China.

Uses
Forrest's Fir makes an excellent, quick-growing specimen tree, suitable for planting singly in grass in large or medium gardens.

Description
Dimensions   Ultimate size rarely exceeds 10.5–12m (35–40ft) high by 3.5–4.5m (12–15ft) wide.
Rate of growth   Rapid when young, usually slowing later, but remaining rapid under good conditions.
Life span   Experience of longevity and ultimate size is limited, as Forrest's Fir was discovered only in this century, but trees can be expected to live in excess of 40 years.
Habit   Pyramidal, with stiffly ascending branches which have bright red or orange shoots when young.
Leaves   Glossy dark green on the upper surface with silvery white reverse.

Flowers   Inconspicuous.
Fruits   Blue-purple cones, about 90mm (3½in.) long by 45mm (1¾in.) wide.
Bark   Concealed by foliage.

Features
This tree provides year-round interest, is quick-growing and does not seem to have any bad traits.
Pollution   Moderately tolerant.
Non-poisonous.

Variety
Although some nurseries list varieties of *Abies delavayi,* most authorities consider that *A. d. forrestii* is the main representative of the species in cultivation.

Requirements
Position   Forrest's Fir grows best in a sheltered situation in a lowland area with a mild temperate climate and moderate rainfall. Cold, frosty, exposed sites should by avoided.

Soil   A deep, fertile, well drained loam that is acid or neutral, pH 6–7, is near the ideal. An occasional late spring feed of general fertilizer ensures steady growth. A top dressing of 70g per sq. m (2oz. per sq. yd) is adequate for normal purposes.

Notes on culture
Planting   Plant small trees, about 300m (1ft) high, in autumn or late spring. Staking and tying is not necessary for small plants, but larger trees need support until firmly rooted. Keep the ground weed-free and mulched within a 450mm (1½ft) radius of young plants.
Space   Allow a minimum area of 7.5m (25ft) diameter at maturity, and avoid planting closer to buildings than 12m (40ft).
Pruning   Prune to limit main shoots to one central leader, and cut back any damaged, diseased or untidy shoots to maintain a good shape. All pruning should be done in spring.
Plant associations   Where space and soil allow, rhododendrons look well with this fir.

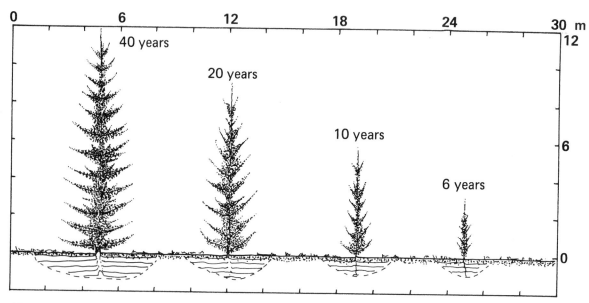

Pest and disease control When given good cultivation Forrest's Fir does not as a rule suffer much from pests or diseases. Adelges, apparent by waxy white tufts on branches, can be controlled by HCH sprays. Aphids, which occasionally attack shoot tips, can be controlled by malathion sprays. Dieback, resulting in diseased and discoloured foliage, can be controlled by cutting out affected parts and spraying with a copper or thiram fungicide. Rusts, usually causing white pustules on leaves and occasionally 'witches' brooms', can be prevented by spraying young trees in spring with a copper or thiram fungicide.

Propagation By seed sown in spring. Named varieties by grafting in spring.

Season of interest	Winter	Spring	Late spring	Summer	Late summer	Autumn
In full leaf	X					X
Autumn colour						
Flowers						
Fruits		X		X		
Bark and stem			X		X	

The following five characteristics determine to a great extent the amount of attention a specific tree requires.

	When planted	5 years	20 years
Height	300 mm	2·5 m	8·0 m
Width	100 mm	600mm	2·0 m
Root spread	100 mm	1·0 m	3·5 m
Hardiness	C	B	B
Wind-firm	3	2	1

Plant care profile

	Minimum	Average	High
Site needs		X——X	
Soil needs		X——X	
Pruning	X——X		
Staking	X		
Maintenance		X	

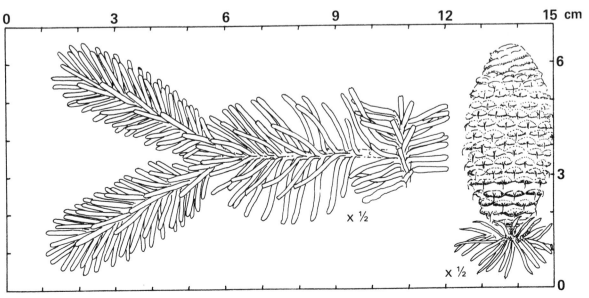

x ½

x ½

Abies koreana – PINACEAE

Korean Fir

A moderately hardy evergreen tree.
Origin Korea.

Uses
The Korean Fir can be used in town as well as country districts, and is effective as a small specimen tree or in a rock garden. The dwarf variety is suitable for planting in beds or rock gardens.

Description
Dimensions Average ultimate size 3–4.5m (10–15ft) high by 2–3m (7–10ft) wide.
Rate of growth Slow.
Life span Trees can be expected to live 40 years or more, but this figure may be revised as experience is gained. The Korean Fir was introduced to cultivation only in this century.
Habit Pyramidal.
Leaves Dark green on the upper surface with white or silver reverse.
Flowers A noteworthy feature. The crimson, pink or green female flowers stand upright on the branches; the male flowers are reddish brown, turning yellow, but less conspicuous among the leaves.

Fruits Green-blue or purple cones, produced when the tree is quite small.
Bark Fairly smooth when young, but concealed by foliage. On old trees rough and fissured.

Features
This Fir provides changing interest throughout the year, with its green and white leaves, coloured flowers and attractive cones. The profusion of cones on even quite small trees can be outstanding.
Pollution Tolerates town pollution better than most firs.
Non-poisonous.

Variety
Abies koreana 'Compact Dwarf'. As the name suggests, a diminutive version of the type.
At present this is the only named variety that can easily be obtained.

Requirements
Position A sunny but sheltered situation in an area with a mild or cool temperate climate suits these trees. Although the Korean Fir is hardy, the new growths can be damaged by frost, so situations subject to late spring frosts should be avoided.

Soil A well drained but moist, light to medium loam that is slightly acid to neutral, pH 6.5–7, will produce the best results.

Notes on culture
Planting Plant small trees, up to 300mm (1ft) high, in autumn or late spring. Staking and tying is not necessary in normal planting. Keep the ground around young plants weed-free and mulched.
Space Allow a minimum area of 3m (10ft) diameter at maturity, and avoid planting closer to buildings than 4.5m (15ft).
Pruning Prune to limit main shoots to one central leader, and cut back any damaged, diseased or untidy shoots to maintain a good shape. All pruning should be done in spring.
Plant associations The Korean Fir can provide an attractive centre piece in an island bed, surrounded by dwarf azaleas.
A.k. 'Compact Dwarf' may be planted among other pygmy conifers, or with rock plants.

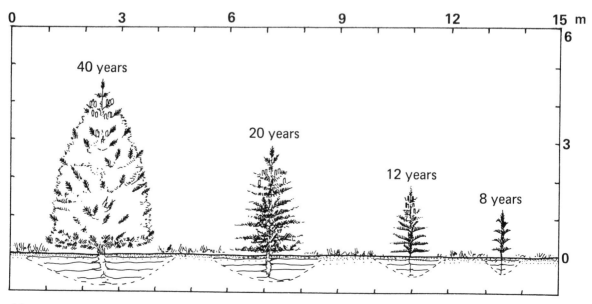

Pest and disease control Adelges, which are conspicuous by their covering of whitish tufts when present, can be controlled by spraying with HCH preparations. Dieback, resulting in diseased and discoloured foliage, can be controlled by cutting out affected parts and spraying with a copper or thiram fungicide. Rusts may appear as white pustules on leaves: to control, avoid overcrowding, and if necessary spray with a copper or thiram fungicide.

Propagation By seed sown in spring. Named varieties by grafting in spring.

Season of interest	Winter	Spring	Late spring	Summer	Late summer	Autumn
In full leaf	X—					—X
Autumn colour						
Flowers			X—X			
Fruits	—X			X—		
Bark and stem						

The following five characteristics determine to a great extent the amount of attention a specific tree requires.

	When planted	5 years	20 years
Height	300 mm	750 mm	3·0 m
Width	100 mm	300 mm	1·5 m
Root spread	100 mm	400 mm	2·0 m
Hardiness	C	B	B
Wind-firm	2	2	1

Plant care profile

	Minimum Average High
Site needs	X———X
Soil needs	X———X
Pruning	X———X
Staking	X
Maintenance	X———X

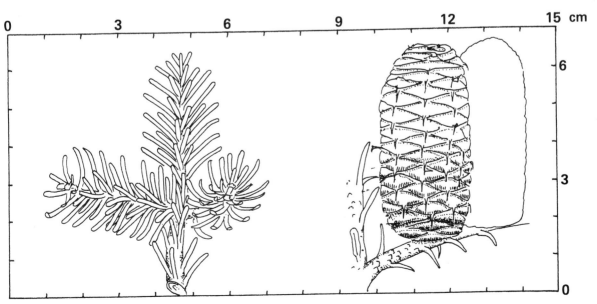

Abies lasiocarpa – PINECEAE
Alpine Fir, Rocky Mountain Fir

A hardy evergreen tree.
Origin Northern USA.

Uses
The true Alpine Fir is less widely planted than its varieties, as, although it makes a fine tree in its home surroundings, it is rather unpredictable in habit and growth. The named varieties do not share this disadvantage. However, *A. lasiocarpa* can be used to advantage as a specimen tree in medium to large gardens. The dwarf type, *A.l.* 'Compacta', is excellent in small gardens or rock gardens.

Description
Dimensions Ultimate size rarely exceeds 12–15m (40–50ft) high by 6–7.5m (20–25ft) wide in gardens.
Rate of growth Usually slow.
Life span Variable, but trees can be expected to live for 60 years or more.
Habit Upright to broadly pyramidal in general outline, but the top third is conical, tapering to a point. The tree becomes flat-topped and spreading with age.
Leaves A pleasing grey-green, and carried on erect branches.

Flowers Inconspicuous.
Fruits Cones which are usually darkish purple in colour, and about 50–100mm (2–4in.) long.
Bark Not particularly noteworthy, except in the variety *A.l. arizonica.*

Features
This fir needs adequate space for growth, and is somewhat temperamental, unlike the dwarf type which is usually reliable.
Pollution Fairly tolerant.
Non-poisonous.

Varieties
Abies lasiocarpa arizonica. Distinctive for its thick, corky, yellowish bark. Foliage of a more intense grey than the species.
Abies lasiocarpa 'Compacta'. A more dwarf type, rarely exceeding 2.5m (8ft) high by 1m (3½ft) wide. Grey-green leaves.

Requirements
Position A sunny or lightly shaded situation in a lowland area with a moist mild or cool temperate climate suits these trees. They need protection from freezing winds and late spring frosts.

Soil A deep, well drained but moist loam that is slightly acid to neutral, pH 6.5–7, should give good results. Apply an annual top dressing of general fertilizer at the rate of 70g per sq. m (2oz. per sq. yd) in late spring.

Notes on culture
Planting Plant small trees, about 300mm (1ft) high, in autumn or late spring. Staking and tying is not necessary for small plants, but larger trees need support until firmly rooted. Keep the ground weed-free and mulched within a 450mm (1½ft) radius of young plants.
Space Allow the Alpine Fir and *A. l. arizonica* a minimum area of 7.5m (25ft) diameter at maturity, and avoid planting closer to buildings than 10m (33ft). Dwarf varieties need proportionately less space.
Pruning Prune to limit main shoots to one central leader, and cut back any damaged, diseased or untidy shoots to maintain a good shape. All pruning should be done in spring.

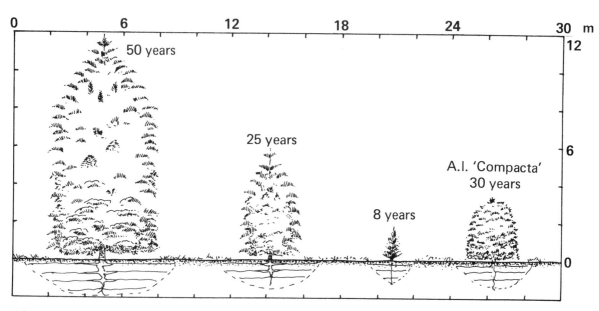

Plant associations When small, the type can be effectively grown with ground cover plants such as Hypericum and Mahonia – as fillers.

A.l. 'Compacta' looks well when planted among other dwarf conifers, or with heathers or rock plants.

Pest and disease control Adelges, apparent by waxy white tufts on branches, can be controlled by HCH sprays. Dieback can usually be kept in check by removing affected parts; if necessary spray with a copper of thiram fungicide. Rusts, which occur as white pustules on leaves, can be controlled by copper or thiram sprays.

Propagation By seed sown in spring. Named varieties by grafting in spring.

Season of interest	Winter	Spring	Late spring	Summer	Late summer	Autumn
In full leaf	X					X
Autumn colour						
Flowers						
Fruits		X		X		
Bark and stem						

The following five characteristics determine to a great extent the amount of attention a specific tree requires.

	When planted	5 years	20 years
Height	300mm	1·5 m	6·0 m
Width	100mm	500mm	2·0 m
Root spread	100mm	1·0 m	3·0 m
Hardiness	C	C	B
Wind-firm	3	2	1

Plant care profile

	Minimum	Average	High
Site needs		X	
Soil needs		X	
Pruning	X	X	
Staking	X	X	
Maintenance	X	X	

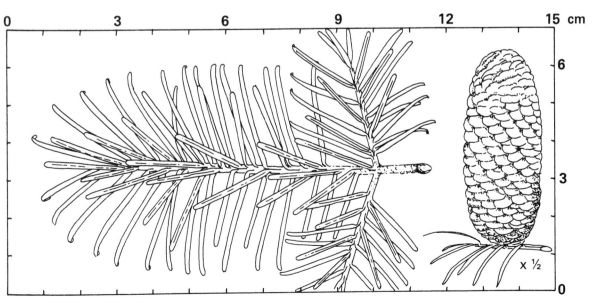

x ½

Abies pinsapo – PINACEAE
Spanish Fir

A moderately hardy evergreen tree.
Origin Southern Spain.

Uses
The Spanish Fir and its varieties are excellent for planting as specimen trees, but are more suitable for large or medium gardens than for small ones.

Description
Dimensions Average ultimate size 10–12m (33–40ft) high by 5–6m (17–20ft) wide but under ideal conditions larger trees can be produced.
Rate of growth Moderate to slow.
Life span This Fir can be expected to live in excess of 50 years.
Habit Pyramidal, with rigid branches radiating in tiers from the main stem. Trees become flat-topped with age, and branches spread out.
Leaves Dark green, thickly arranged around the brownish shoots, which have reddish buds.
Flowers Insignificant.
Fruits Purple-brown cones, about 100–125mm (4–5in) long by 40mm (1½in) wide.
Bark Inconspicuous, and furrowed.

Features
The Spanish Fir provides year-round interest, is reliable and adaptable, and can be used on a range of differing sites. An attractive tree, and excellent for alkaline or chalk soils. Usually well rooted and wind firm.
Pollution Moderately resistant.
Non-poisonous.

Varieties
Abies pinsapo 'Aurea'. A paler-leaved form, and less vigorous than the true Spanish Fir.
Abies pinsapo 'Glauca'. Blue-grey leaves.

Requirements
Position A warm or mild temperate climate suits these trees. They grow best in warm, sunny but sheltered situations, protected from cold north and east winds and spring frosts.
Soil A well drained, light or medium loam that is neutral or alkaline, pH 7–7.5 is ideal. The Spanish Fir is one of the best conifers for chalk or limestone soils.

Notes on culture
Planting Plant small trees, about 300mm (1ft) high. Autumn is the best time for planting, especially if the soil is light and well drained, but if necessary trees can be moved in spring. Staking and tying is not necessary for small plants, but larger trees need support until firmly rooted.
Space Allow a minimum area of 6m (20ft) diameter at maturity. Avoid planting closer to dwellings than 7.5m (25ft), and give more space if possible, as this tree casts fairly heavy shade.
Pruning Prune to limit main shoots to one central leader. Some trimming to maintain shape may be done, but in general the less cutting the better. All pruning should be done in spring.
Plant associations Viburnums and chalk plants grow well with this fir.

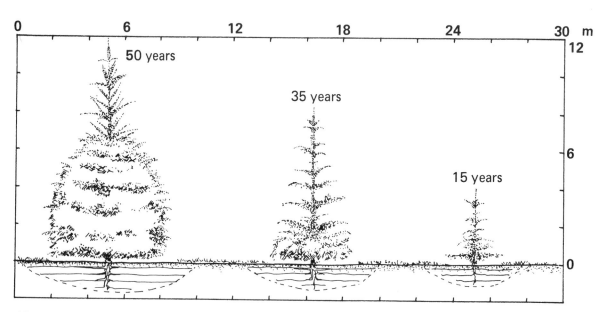

Conifers provide wide scope to a garden designer, offering a rich variety of colour, shape and texture. Groups like this, in subtle shades of green, blue and gold, are attractive at all times of the year. The blue Cedar background contrasts well with the small, rounded yellowish green *Thuya* 'Rosedalis', in the centre

Groups of fastigiate, conical and rounded trees can be used in many situations, large or small. Here an element of seasonal change is introduced by using one or two broad-leaved trees to provide soft shades of spring green

A framework of conifers provides an excellent setting for summer bedding. The fastigiate Irish Juniper in the centre, flanked by conical varieties of *Chamaecyparis* form a distinctive background

Pest and disease control Adelges, which can cause pineapple-like galls accompanied by waxy white tufts, can usually be controlled by HCH sprays. Rusts may appear as white pustules on leaves: to control, avoid overcrowding, and if necessary spray with a copper or thiram fungicide.
Propagation By seed sown in spring. Named varieties by grafting in spring.

Season of interest	Winter	Spring	Late spring	Summer	Late summer	Autumn
In full leaf	X———					———X
Autumn colour						
Flowers						
Fruits	———X				X———	
Bark and stem						

The following five characteristics determine to a great extent the amount of attention a specific tree requires.

	When planted	5 years	20 years
Height	300 mm	1·5 m	6·0 m
Width	100 mm	500 mm	2·5 m
Root spread	100 mm	1·0 m	3·0 m
Hardiness	C	C	B/C
Wind-firm	3	2	1

Plant care profile

	Minimum Average High
Site needs	X———X
Soil needs	X
Pruning	X———X
Staking	X———X
Maintenance	X

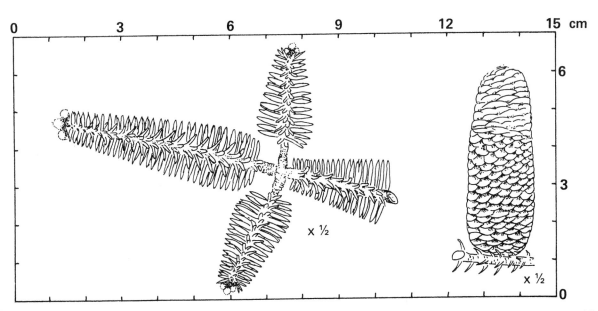

x ½

x ½

Calocedrus decurrens – CUPRESSACEAE
Incense Cedar

A moderately hardy evergreen tree, better known by its former name of *Libocedrus decurrens*.
Origin   California and Oregon.

Uses
The Incense Cedar, with its rather symmetrical shape, is suitable for formal gardens. It is outstanding as a single specimen set on a lawn or in grass.

Description
Dimensions   Average ultimate size 12–15m (40–50ft) high by 1.5–2m (5–7ft) wide.
Rate of growth   Slow.
Life span   This tree should live for 100 years or more.
Habit   Usually narrow and columnar in temperate areas, but wider, more conical forms occur in Mediterranean regions.
Leaves   Dark green. The foliage is, as a rule, retained almost to ground level even with old specimens.
Flowers   Inconspicuous.
Fruits   Narrowly ovoid yellowish cones, about 25mm (1in.) long and borne in clusters.
Bark   Pale red or reddish brown, often concealed beneath upward-growing branches.

Features
Provided that climate, soil and site are suitable, this tree will provide years of trouble-free pleasure and satisfaction.
Pollution   Tolerant.
Non-poisonous.

Variety
Calocedrus decurrens 'Aureovariegata'. A very useful garden tree. Similar in habit to the Incense Cedar, but slower-growing and wider. Gold-splashed foliage. Average size 9–12m (30–40ft) high by 3m (10ft) wide.

Requirements
Position   A sunny but sheltered situation in a lowland area with a warm or mild temperate climate suits these trees. They need protection from cold and freezing winds.
Soil   A deep, fertile, well drained but moist loam that is neutral, pH around 7, should give good results.

Notes on culture
Planting   Plant small trees, up to 600mm (2ft) high, in autumn or late spring. Staking and tying is not necessary for small plants, but larger trees need support until firmly rooted. Keep the ground around young plants weed-free and mulched.
Space   Although this tree is of a narrow, columnar habit, it needs space to be seen to best effect. Allow a minimum area of 4.5m (15ft) diameter at maturity, and avoid planting closer to buildings than 6m (20ft).
Pruning   Prune to limit main shoots to one central leader. Some trimming to maintain shape may be done, but in general the less cutting the better. Any pruning should be carried out in late spring.
Plant associations   Seen to best effect in grass.
Pest and disease control   Rarely necessary.
Propagation   Can be by seed sown in autumn, but as there is some variation among seedlings other means may be preferable. Tip cuttings about 75mm (3in.) long, taken mid- to late summer, can be rooted under frames and grown on.

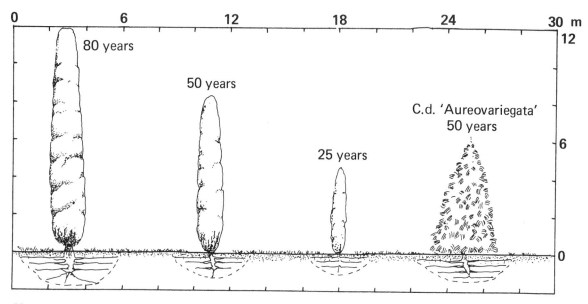

0   6   12   18   24   30 m

80 years

50 years

25 years

C.d. 'Aureovariegata'
50 years

12

6

0

Season of interest	Winter	Spring	Late spring	Summer	Late summer	Autumn
In full leaf	X————					————X
Autumn colour						
Flowers						
Fruits	——X				X——	
Bark and stem						

The following five characteristics determine to a great extent the amount of attention a specific tree requires.

	When planted	5 years	20 years
Height	600 mm	1·5 m	5·0 m
Width	100 mm	150 mm	600 mm
Root spread	150 mm	250 mm	1·0 m
Hardiness	C	B/C	B/C
Wind-firm	3	2	1

Plant care profile

	Minimum	Average	High
Site needs		X	
Soil needs		X	
Pruning	X————	—X	
Staking	X————	—X	
Maintenance	X————	—X	

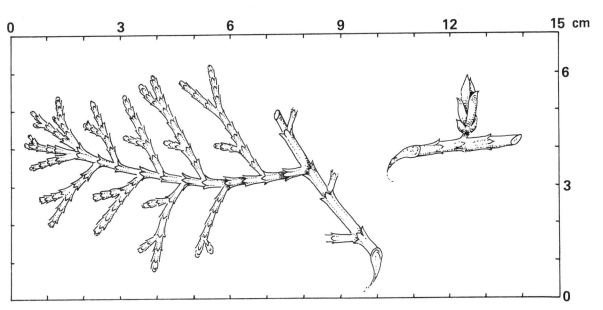

Cedrus atlantica – PINACEAE
Atlas Cedar

A moderately hardy evergreen tree.
Origin Algeria and Morocco.

Uses
The Atlas Cedar and its varieties all make imposing specimen trees, but with the exception of *C.a.* 'Aurea' they are best suited to large gardens. A formal setting is the most appropriate.

Description
Dimensions Average ultimate size 15–18m (50–60ft) high by 6–7.5m (20–25ft) wide.
Rate of growth Slow, increasing to moderate and occasionally to rapid when established, becoming slow again as trees reach maturity.
Life span Trees often live 150 years, and can considerably exceed this.
Habit Pyramidal when young, becoming more spreading with age, but retaining a leading shoot.
Leaves Dark green, single on new shoots but in groups of 20–30 or more on older growths.
Flowers Tassle-like male flowers appear on the upper surface of shoots and branches of mature trees in late summer. Female flowers are inconspicuous.

Fruits Blue-green cones, about 75–100mm (3–4in.) long.
Bark Rough and grey, with brownish furrows.

Features
The Atlas Cedar and its varieties make very distinguished garden trees. They seem to have very few faults once established, and they require little by way of attention.
Pollution Only fairly tolerant.
Non-poisonous.

Varieties
Cedrus atlantica 'Aurea'. Much smaller than the type, rarely exceeding 4.5m (15ft) high. Golden yellow foliage.
Cedrus atlantica 'Fastigiata'. A slightly shorter tree than the type, and much narrower, about 2–3m (7–10ft) wide. Grey-blue foliage.
Cedrus atlantica glauca. An outstanding variety, with blue-green foliage and, at maturity, blue cones.
Cedrus atlantica 'Glauca Pendula'. Bluish grey-green foliage and pendulous branches.

Requirements
Position A sunny but sheltered situation in an area with a warm or mild temperate climate suits these trees best.
Soil A deep, well drained, light to medium loam that is neutral, pH 7, is the most suitable, but alkaline soils are tolerated.

Notes on culture
Planting Plant small trees, 300–450mm (1–1½ft) high, in autumn or late spring. Staking and tying is sometimes necessary for small plants, and trees over 900mm (3ft) high, and all pendulous forms, need support until firmly rooted. Keep the ground around young plants weed-free and mulched.
Space This tree needs room to develop, so allow a minimum area of 7.5m (25ft) diameter at maturity. To prevent excessive shade, avoid planting closer to dwellings than 9m (30ft).
Pruning Prune to limit main shoots to one central leader until the required height is reached. Old, worn out branches can be cut off flush with the stem. All pruning should be done in spring.

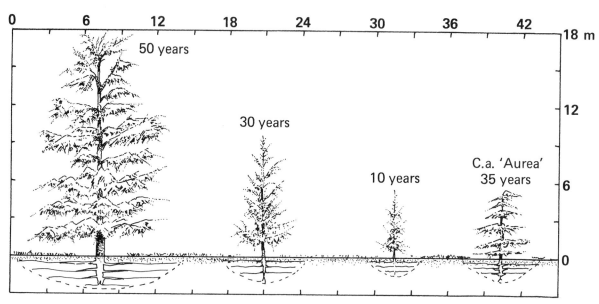

Plant associations Best with other conifers. Underplanting except with bulbs is not very satisfactory.

Pest and disease control Rarely necessary, but occasionally honey fungus attacks these trees. If planting on land which may have been contaminated, first remove all old tree stumps and sterilize the soil with formaldehyde. Allow the formaldehyde fumes to dissipate from the soil before planting; this normally takes four to six weeks.

Propagation By seed sown in spring. Named varieties, which do not come true from seed, by grafting in spring.

Season of interest	Winter	Spring	Late spring	Summer	Late summer	Autumn
In full leaf	X					X
Autumn colour						
Flowers					X—X	
Fruits	X		X			
Bark and stem						

The following five characteristics determine to a great extent the amount of attention a specific tree requires.

	When planted	5 years	20 years
Height	450 mm	2·0 m	7·5 m
Width	250 mm	1·0 m	3·0 m
Root spread	200 mm	1·5 m	4·5 m
Hardiness	C	B/C	B
Wind-firm	3	2	1

Plant care profile

	Minimum Average High
Site needs	X———X
Soil needs	X
Pruning	X
Staking	X
Maintenance	X———X

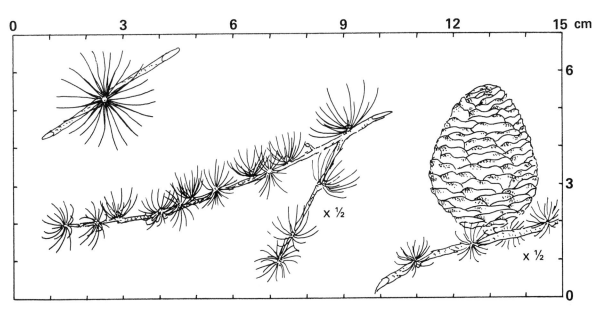

x ½

x ½

0   3   6   9   12   15 cm

6

3

0

53

Cedrus deodara – PINACEAE
Deodar, Deodar Cedar

A moderately hardy evergreen tree.
Origin Himalayas.

Uses
The true Deodar makes an excellent specimen tree for the large or medium garden. The dwarf varieties may be used in mixed plantings, or to add height in a rock garden.

Description
Dimensions Variable according to conditions, average ultimate size 13.5–18m (45–60ft) high by 4.5–6m (15–20ft) wide, but can grow much larger.
Rate of growth Slow at first, increasing to moderate.
Life span These trees can live 150 years or more.
Habit Pyramidal when young, becoming flat-topped with age. The branch tips are pendulous.
Leaves Variable in colour, but usually blue-grey.
Flowers Not very conspicuous.
Fruits Cones which are usually light brown, and about 100mm (4in.) long by 75mm (3in.) wide. Rarely borne by trees under 40 years old.
Bark Rough, grey-brown.

Features
The Deodar is most attractive as a specimen or garden tree in the young state, as the lower branches start to deteriorate in later years.
Pollution Fairly tolerant.
Non-poisonous.

Varieties
Cedrus deodara 'Aurea' (Golden Deodar). Less hardy, slower-growing and smaller than the type, rarely exceeding 4–5m (13–17ft) high. The foliage is at its brightest yellow in spring.
Cedrus deodara 'Aurea Pendula'. A weeping form. Yellow foliage.
Cedrus deodara 'Pendula'. A very pendulous form; the central stem needs supporting if this conifer is to grow upwards as well as outwards. Approximate ultimate size 900mm–1.2m (3–4ft) high by 2m (7ft) wide.
Cedrus deodara 'Verticillata Glauca'. A smaller tree than the type. Forms a thickly branched mass of grey foliage.

Requirements
Position The Deodar is the most tender Cedar, and requires a warm temperate climate. Sunny, dryish situations or sheltered coastal sites are most favourable to good colour and growth. In frost-prone sites young trees grow better in the light shade of shelter trees.
Soil A warm, well drained loam that is neutral, pH around 7, is most suitable.

Notes on culture
Planting Plant small trees, 300–450mm (1–1½ft) high, in autumn or late spring. A hessian wrapping round the trunk, or some other form of protection from wind, is necessary on cold or frosty sites. Keep the ground weed-free and mulched within a 600mm (2ft) radius of young plants.
Space Although this tree is of a narrow, columnar habit, it needs space to be seen to best effect. Allow a minimum area of 4.5m (15ft) diameter at maturity, and avoid planting closer to buildings than 6m (20ft).

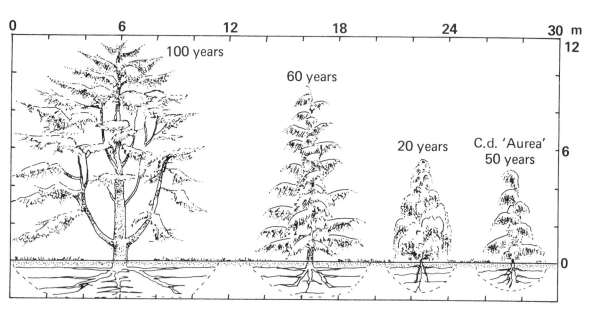

Pruning Prune to limit main shoots to one central leader. Cut back any damaged, diseased or untidy shoots to maintain a good shape; the lower branches of old trees can be cut out as the boughs become unsightly. All pruning should be done in spring.
Plant associations Best with other conifers or alone for maximum effect.
Pest and desease control Rarely necessary.
Propagation By seed sown in spring. Named varieties by grafting in spring.

Season of interest	Winter	Spring	Late spring	Summer	Late summer	Autumn
In full leaf	X————					————X
Autumn colour						
Flowers						
Fruits	——X			X————		
Bark and stem						

The following five characteristics determine to a great extent the amount of attention a specific tree requires.

	When planted	5 years	20 years
Height	450 mm	1·5 m	6·0 m
Width	250 mm	750 mm	2·5 m
Root spread	200 mm	1·0 m	3·5 m
Hardiness	C	C	C
Wind-firm	3	2	2

Plant care profile

	Minimum Average High
Site needs	X————X
Soil needs	X
Pruning	X
Staking	X————X
Maintenance	X

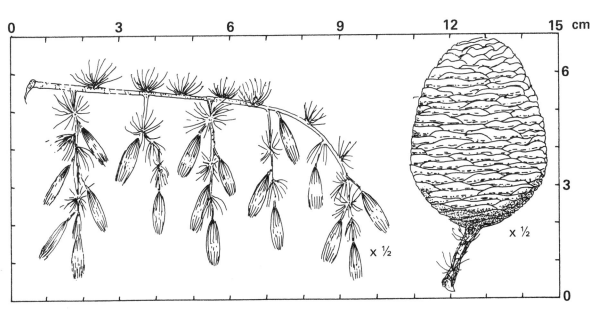

x ½

x ½

Cedrus libani – PINACEAE
Cedar of Lebanon, Lebanon Cedar

A moderately hardy evergreen tree.
Origin   Lebanon, Syria and south-eastern Turkey.

Uses
The true Cedar of Lebanon makes an impressive specimen tree for the large garden, especially when it is planted in grass. The dwarf varieties are effective in small gardens or rock gardens, and generally in confined spaces unsuitable for large trees.

Description
Dimensions   Average ultimate size 12–15m (40–50ft) high by 7.5–9m (25–30ft) wide.
Rate of growth   Slow to moderate.
Life span   Under good conditions these trees can live upwards of 300 years.
Habit   Narrowly pyramidal when young, spreading with age.
Leaves   Dark green, some with bluish tints.
Flowers   Inconspicuous.
Fruits   Roughly barrel-shaped cones, 75–125mm (3–5in.) long and half as wide, and bluish-green at first, later turning brown.
Bark   Rugged, grey-brown.

Features
The Cedar of Lebanon forms a stately large tree when mature. The thick trunks of older trees are quite a feature, as are the larger lower limbs. Severe damage by heavy snowfalls can cause large lower branches to snap off.
Pollution   Moderately tolerant.
Non-poisonous.

Varieties
Cedrus libani 'Nana'. A very compact, slow-growing form rarely more than 1.5–1.8m (5–6ft) high by 750mm–1.2m (2½–4ft) wide.
Cedrus libani 'Sargentii'. A very dwarf, slow-growing conifer which forms a mound of green, drooping foliage.

Requirements
Position   The largest and finest specimens are to be found in sunny and dry locations in warm temperate regions. Mild temperate areas are also suitable. Areas subject to heavy snowfalls are best avoided.
Soil   A deep, well drained but moist loam that is neutral, pH around 7, is close to the ideal.

Notes on culture
Planting   Plant small trees, 300–450mm (1–1½ft) high, in autumn or late spring. Staking and tying is often necessary for small plants, and trees over 900mm (3ft) high need support until firmly rooted.
Space   This tree requires considerable room to develop, so allow a minimum area of 9m (30ft) diameter at maturity, and avoid planting closer to buildings than 14m (45ft). Dwarf forms need little space.
Pruning   Prune to limit main shoots to one central leader until the required height is reached. Subsequent requirements are negligible, until the lower branches become thin and worn out in old age. These can then gradually be cut back flush to the main stem. The wounds should be painted over to prevent disease organisms gaining entry. All pruning should be done in spring.

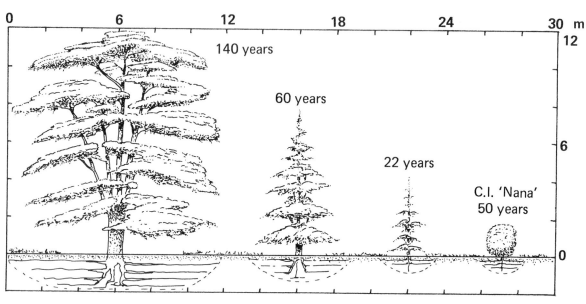

140 years

60 years

22 years

C.I. 'Nana'
50 years

Plant associations   Most effective with other conifers or on its own. The dwarf varieties may be planted among other small conifers, or with heathers or rock plants.
Pest and disease control   Rarely necessary.
Propagation   By seed sown in spring. Named varieties by grafting in spring.

Season of interest	Winter	Spring	Late spring	Summer	Late summer	Autumn
In full leaf	X—					—X
Autumn colour						
Flowers						
Fruits		X			X—	
Bark and stem	X—					—X

The following five characteristics determine to a great extent the amount of attention a specific tree requires.

	When planted	5 years	20 years
Height	450 mm	1·2 m	4·5 m
Width	250 mm	600 mm	2·0 m
Root spread	250 mm	900 mm	3·0 m
Hardiness	C	C	B/C
Wind-firm	3	2/3	2/3

Plant care profile

	Minimum Average High
Site needs	X——X
Soil needs	X——X
Pruning	X
Staking	X———X
Maintenance	X——X

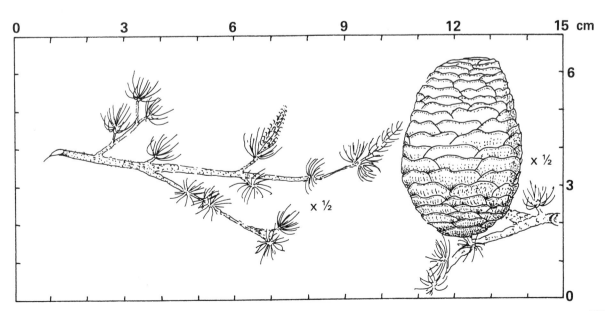

x ½   x ½

Cephalotaxus harringtonia – CEPHALOTAXACEAE
Plum Yew

A hardy evergreen tree or shrub.
Origin China and Japan.

Uses
The Plum Yew and its varieties are useful for planting in small gardens and in shaded parts of rock gardens.

Description
Dimensions Ultimate size rarely exceeds 2.5–3.5m (8–12ft) high by 2–3m (7–10ft) wide in cultivation.
Rate of growth Slow.
Life span Variable, but healthy specimens can live 40 years or more.
Habit Rounded when young, becoming more upright and domed with age. The stem is usually erect, with branches, which terminate in pale green tips, arranged in tiers.
Leaves Resembling those of Yew, but longer, and dark green on the upper surface with grey-green reverse.
Flowers Small and inconspicuous.
Fruits Green, plum-like fruits, 25–30mm (1–1¼in.) long by 15mm(¾in.) wide, which earn this tree its name.
Bark Concealed by foliage.

Features
The Plum Yew is an attractive conifer which requires very little attention, being almost trouble-free. The arching, young green shoots of the 'Cow's Tail Pine' variety are unusual and stand out to catch one's notice.
Pollution Tolerant.
Non-poisonous.

Varieties
Cephalotaxus harringtonia drupacea. A form with pronounced arching light green tips to the shoots. These have earned this conifer the name of 'Cow's Tail Pine'.
Cephalotaxus harringtonia 'Fastigiata'. A form which resembles the Irish Yew in its narrow and upright habit. Leaves a darker green than those of the type.

Requirements
Position A sheltered, lightly shaded situation in an area with a mild temperate climate suits these conifers, which can tolerate both sun and shade.

Soil A well drained loam, preferably fairly moist, is suitable. These plants can grow satisfactorily on land ranging from slightly acid to slightly alkaline, pH 6.5–7.5.

Notes on culture
Planting Plant small conifers, preferably not more than 300–450mm (1–1½ft) high, in autumn or late spring. Staking and tying is not necessary.
Space Allow each plant a minimum area of 900mm–1.2m (3–4ft) at maturity. Where groups of two or more of the same type are planted together the distance between can be reduced to 600–900mm (2–3ft). Avoid planting too close to windows unless the conifers are to be clipped.
Pruning Where single-stem trees are wanted prune to limit main shoots to one central leader. On all types cut back any damaged, diseased or untidy shoots to maintain a good shape. All pruning should be done in spring.

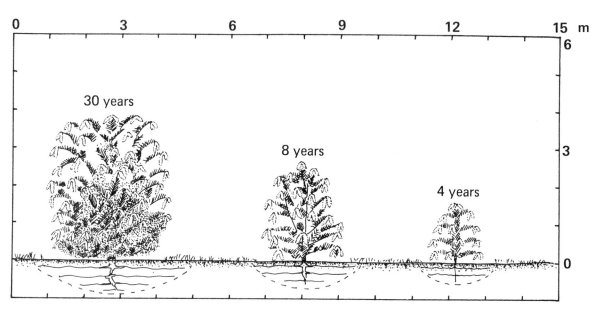

Plant associations These plants look well in mixed beds of conifers, and when planted beneath broad-leaved trees.

Pest and disease control Rarely necessary.

Propagation By seed sown in spring or late summer. Named varieties by cuttings taken in late summer.

Season of interest	Winter	Spring	Late spring	Summer	Late summer	Autumn
In full leaf	X					X
Autumn colour						
Flowers						
Fruits			X	X		
Bark and stem						

The following five characteristics determine to a great extent the amount of attention a specific tree requires.

	When planted	5 years	20 years
Height	450 mm	1·2 m	3·0 m
Width	450 mm	1·2 m	3·0 m
Root spread	450 mm	1·5 m	4·0 m
Hardiness	C	C	B
Wind-firm	2	1	1

Plant care profile

	Minimum	Average	High
Site needs		X	
Soil needs		X	
Pruning	X		
Staking	X		
Maintenance	X		

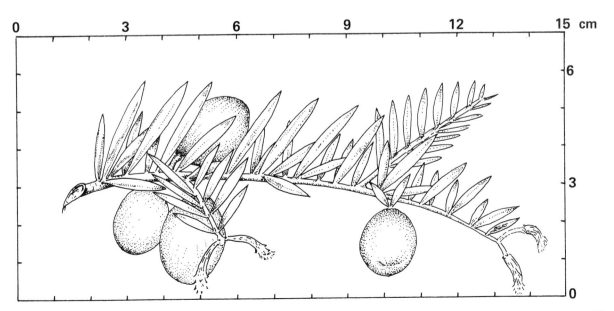

Chamaecyparis lawsoniana – CUPRESSACEAE
Lawson Cypress, English Cypress

A hardy evergreen tree.
Origin Japan, Formosa and USA.

Uses
The true Lawson Cypress makes an excellent specimen tree, screen or shelter for the larger garden. The taller varieties are also very good as individual specimens or when planted in groups. The dwarf forms are eminently suitable for use in mixed plantings, in beds or in rock gardens.

Description
Dimensions Average ultimate size in gardens 12–13.5m (40–45ft) high by 3–4m (10–13ft) wide. Trees in the wild can almost double these figures.
Rate of growth In the species moderate to rapid, but in most of the varieties slow to moderate.
Life span Trees of 100 years old are quite common.
Habit Variable from narrowly fastigiate to broadly pyramidal.
Leaves Flattened scales, varying in colour from dark green to greys and blue-greens.
Flowers Sometimes gives pinkish haze in spring.

Fruits Small rounded cones, turning brown when ripe, and about 8mm (⅓in.) in diameter.
Bark Warm reddish brown.

Features
Lawson Cypress is one of the most popular of all evergreen trees, and has few if any serious faults. Very hardy and windfirm in most gardens.
Pollution Moderately resistant.
Non-poisonous.

Varieties
This Cypress has given rise to numerous kinds of garden-worthy conifers. The following are some of the most outstanding.
Chamaecyparis lawsoniana 'Allumii'. Upright blue-grey growth, tapering to a point.
Chamaecyparis lawsoniana 'Columnaris'. A column of blue-touched grey foliage.
Chamaecyparis lawsoniana 'Ellwoodii'. An upright blue-green column, tapering at base and top.
Chamaecyparis lawsoniana 'Ellwood's Gold'. Similar to *C.l.* 'Ellwoodii', but foliage is touched with yellow.

Chamaecyparis lawsoniana 'Erecta'. Narrow and erect green pyramid.
Chamaecyparis lawsoniana 'Erecta Aurea'. A golden form of *C.l.* 'Erecta'.
Chamaecyparis lawsoniana 'Lanei'. A form with a pyramidal, compact habit and golden foliage.
Chamaecyparis lawsoniana 'Lutea'. A form with pyramidal, upright growth and yellow and green leaves.
Chamaecyparis lawsoniana 'Minima Aurea'. A slow-growing, compact dwarf form, suitable for the rock garden.
Chamaecyparis lawsoniana 'Minima Glauca'. A very slow-growing, sea green version of *C.l.* 'Minima Aurea'.
Chamaecyparis lawsoniana 'Pottenii'. A form with a pyramidal or upright habit and dense, compact, feathery foliage.
Chamaecyparis lawsoniana 'Stewartii'. Similar to *C.l.* 'Lanei', but more golden than yellow.
Chamaecyparis lawsoniana 'Wisselii'. A form with a pyramidal habit and twisted, bluish-green leaves.

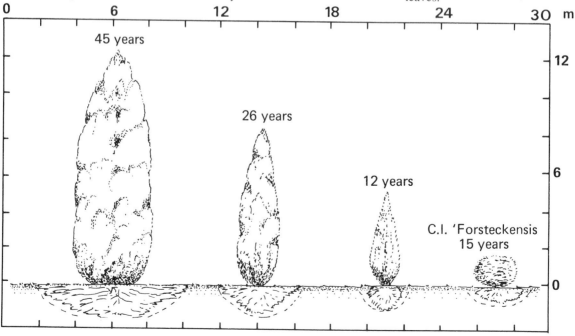

Requirements

Position A moist mild or cool temperate climate suits this conifer. It grows well in sun or shade, but the gold, yellow and blue varieties colour best in full sun. Most of the varieties need protection from cold and freezing north or east winds.

Soil A deep, well drained but moist loam that is slightly acid to neutral, pH 6.5–7, is ideal, but slightly alkaline chalk soils are tolerated.

Notes on culture

Planting Plant small trees, preferably not more than 450mm (1½ft) high, in autumn or spring. Staking and tying is not usually necessary for small plants, but some varieties, such as *C.l.* 'Erecta', need tying in to prevent branches from spreading out.

Space With upright pyramidal trees the roots usually extend well beyond the drip line in search of food and moisture. Allow the true Lawson Cypress a minimum area of 4m (13ft) diameter at maturity and a similar distance from buildings. Dwarf forms and the slower-growing varieties need much less, 1.2–1.8m (4–6ft). Temporary plantings may be made closer, and removed as the trees grow.

Pruning Limit the number of main stems to one with tall varieties, but little cutting if any is needed. Prune in spring, this often consists of no more than trimming untidy shoots into shape.

Plant associations This tree mixes well with other conifers and ground-cover plants of all types including *Hypericum calycinum* and Mahonia. The dwarf forms look well among mixed conifers, or with shrubs, heathers or rock plants.

Pest and disease control Rarely necessary, but honey fungus occasionally attacks these trees. If planting on land which may have been contaminated, first remove all old tree stumps and sterilize the soil with formaldehyde. Allow four to six weeks for the formaldehyde fumes to dissipate from the soil before planting.

Propagation By seed sown in spring. Named varieties by cuttings taken in late spring or autumn, or by grafting in spring.

Season of interest	Winter	Spring	Late spring	Summer	Late summer	Autumn
In full leaf	X—					—X
Autumn colour						
Flowers		X—X				
Fruits			—X		X—	
Bark and stem						

The following five characteristics determine to a great extent the amount of attention a specific tree requires.

	When planted	5 years	20 years
Height	450 mm	1·8 m	6·0 m
Width	250 mm	600 mm	2·0 m
Root spread	200 mm	900 mm	3·0 m
Hardiness	B	B	A/B
Wind-firm	3	2	1/2

Plant care profile

	Minimum	Average	High
Site needs		X	
Soil needs		X	
Pruning	X—	—X	
Staking	X		
Maintenance	X		

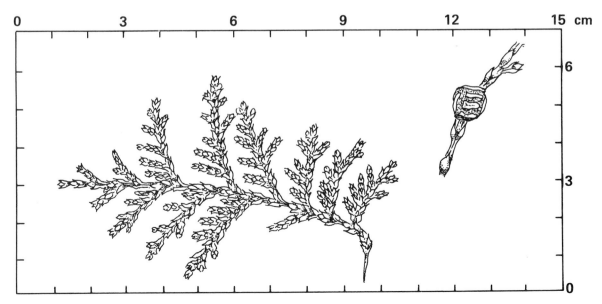

Chamaecyparis nootkatensis – CUPRESSACEAE
Nootka Cypress

A very hardy evergreen tree.
Origin North-western USA.

Uses
The Nootka Cypress is useful for cold sites where less hardy trees would fail. This species and its taller varieties make handsome specimen trees in large or medium gardens. *C.n.* 'Compacta' is ideal as a specimen for the smaller site, as well as being effective in rock gardens.

Description
Dimensions Average ultimate size in gardens about 9–12m (30–40ft) high by 4.5m (15ft) wide. This is only one-third of the size this Cypress can reach in its native surroundings.
Rate of growth Moderate to rapid in the early years, becoming slower with age.
Life span These conifers can be expected to live 50–60 years or more.
Habit A regular, pyramidal shape, slender at first, broadening in proportion to height with age.
Leaves a matt dark green.
Flowers Not usually conspicuous.

Fruits Rounded blue-grey cones about 12mm (½in.) across, ripening in the second year after flowering.
Bark Concealed by foliage.

Features
The Nootka Cypress is attractive in appearance, hardy, wind firm, and requires little attention.
Pollution Tolerant.
Non-poisonous.

Varieties
This Cypress has produced several fine varieties. Some of the best are listed below.
Chamaecyparis nootkatensis 'Compacta'. More rounded in habit than the type, and ultimate height usually not more than about 3m (10ft). Mid-green foliage.
Chamaecyparis nootkatensis 'Glauca'. Can reach about 12m (40ft) high. Sea green foliage.
Chamaecyparis nootkatensis 'Lutea'. Similar to *C.n.* 'Glauca', but with gold or yellow foliage.
Chamaecyparis nootkatensis 'Pendula'. Although this form is slow-growing, and the main shoot needs support initially, it makes a fine pendulous tree.

Requirements
Position An open or lightly shaded situation in an area with a moist cool temperate climate suits these trees. Golden or variegated types are usually better coloured in sunny situations than in the shade.
Soil A well drained, medium loam that is neutral, pH 7, and preferably well supplied with moisture during the summer months, is most suitable. These trees will tolerate acid soils. On poor soils apply a dressing of 70g per sq. m (2oz. per sq. yd) of general fertilizer before planting. and repeat each spring for the first few years.

Notes on culture
Planting Plant small conifers, preferably not more the 450mm (1½ft) high, in autumn or late spring. Staking and tying is not necessary for small plants, but larger ones need support until firmly rooted.

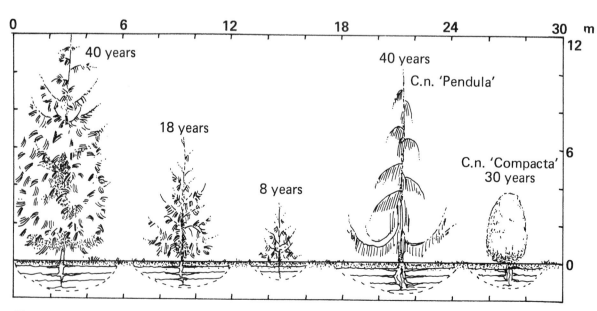

Space Allow the true Nootka Cypress and large varieties a minimum area of about 4.5m (15ft) diameter at maturity, and avoid planting closer to buildings than 7.5m (25ft). Smaller varieties, such as *C.n.* 'Compacta', require an area of 1.5m (5ft) diameter.

Pruning Prune tall forms to limit main shoots to one central leader. On all types cut back any damaged, diseased or untidy shoots to maintain a good shape. All pruning should be done in spring.

Plant associations Looks well with other conifers and when planted around with bulbs and ground cover plants such as berberis.

Pest and disease control Rarely necessary, but occasionally honey fungus attacks these conifers. If planting on land which may have been contaminated, first remove all old tree stumps and sterilize the soil with formaldehyde. Allow four to six weeks for the formaldehyde fumes to dissipate from the soil before planting.

Propagation By seed sown in spring. Named varieties by cuttings taken in late spring or autumn, or by grafting in spring.

Season of interest	Winter	Spring	Late spring	Summer	Late summer	Autumn
In full leaf	X———	———	———	———	———	—X
Autumn colour						
Flowers						
Fruits	—X				X——	———
Bark and stem						

The following five characteristics determine to a great extent the amount of attention a specific tree requires.

	When planted	5 years	20 years
Height	450 mm	1·8 m	6·0 m
Width	250 mm	750 mm	2·5 m
Root spread	200 mm	1·0 m	3·5 m
Hardiness	B	B	A
Wind-firm	2	2	1

Plant care profile

	Minimum	Average	High
Site needs		X	
Soil needs		X	
Pruning	X——	——X	
Staking	X——	——X	
Maintenance	X——	——X	

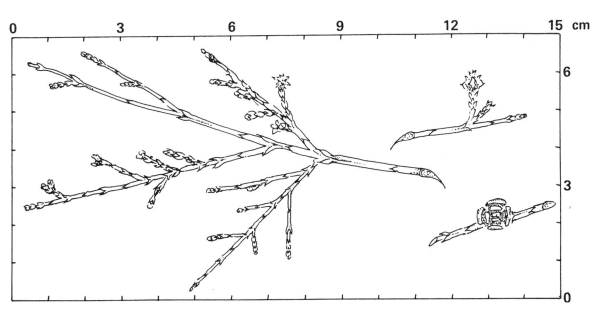

Chamaecyparis obtusa – CUPRESSACEAE
Hinoki Cypress

A hardy evergreen tree or shrub.
Origin Japan.

Uses
The Hinoki Cypress and its taller varieties make handsome specimen trees and also look well in groups as a background in the large or medium garden. The small varieties can be very effective in small gardens and rock gardens.

Description
Dimensions Ultimate size rarely exceeds 9–12m (30–40ft) high by 3–4m (10–13ft) wide in gardens.
Rate of growth Slow.
Life span These conifers start to decline after 40–50 years, especially on shallow, poor soils.
Habit Usually a broadly pyramidal shape which becomes more domed with age.
Leaves Mid-green, with silver reverse. Although individually these are scales, the general appearance is more feathery than that of many conifers.
Flowers Inconspicuous.
Fruits Cones which are rounded and brown when ripe, and usually about 8mm (⅓ in.) across.
Bark On older conifers reddish brown and furrowed.

Features
The Hinoki Cypress can be most attractive throughout its life, until its foliage and branches become thin and bare in old age. It is wind-firm, but has definite preferences with regard to soils and sites.
Pollution Tolerant.
Non-poisonous.

Varieties
C. obtusa has produced many varieties. Some of the best forms are indicated below.
Chamaecyparis obtusa 'Crippsii'. Ultimate size about 6–7.5m (20–25ft) high by 3–4m (10–13ft) wide. Golden yellow foliage and good winter colour.
Chamaecyparis obtusa 'Nana'. A dwarf green ball about 600mm (2ft) in diameter.
Chamaecyparis obtusa 'Nana Aurea'. Similar to *C.o.* 'Nana', but golden yellow.
Chamaecyparis obtusa 'Nana Gracilis'. A rounded form, ultimate size about 3m (10ft) high by 2m (7ft) wide. Green foliage.
Chamaecyparis obtusa 'Pygmaea'. A low green bush ultimately about 1m (3½ft) high by 1.5m (5ft) wide.

Chamaecyparis obtusa 'Tetragona Aurea'. A form which grows to about 5m (17ft) high by 3–4m (10–13ft) wide, producing several main ascending branches. Golden yellow foliage. Needs full sun and is more tender than many varieties.

Requirements
Position A sunny but sheltered situation in an area with a moist warm or mild temperate climate suits these conifers. The coloured varieties need full sun, but can be scorched by cold or drying winds.
Soil A deep, well drained but moist loam that is acid, pH 6–6.5, is most suitable. Chalk or limestone soils should be avoided.

Notes on culture
Planting Plant small conifers, up to 450mm (1½ft) high, in autumn or late spring. Staking and tying is not necessary. Keep the ground around young plants weed-free and mulched.
Space Allow each plant a minimum area of a diameter equal to its width at maturity. The true Hinoki Cypress should not be planted closer to buildings than about 7.5m (25ft).

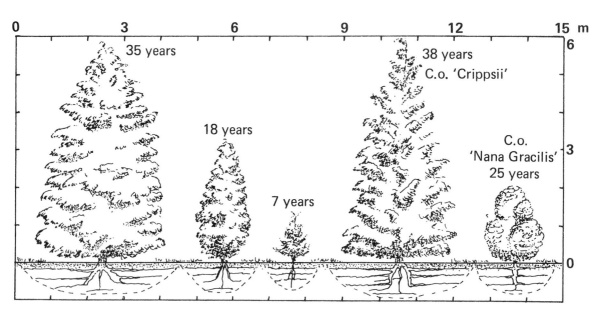

Pruning Prune tall forms to limit main shoots to one central leader. Dwarf conifers need an occasional trim to shorten untidy shoots and keep plants in good shape, and on all types the odd trim may be needed to thicken up thinly leaved areas. All pruning should be done in spring.

Plant associations The small varieties look well in groups of mixed dwarf conifers, among small shrubs, or with heathers or rock plants.

Pest and disease control Rarely necessary.

Propagation By seed sown in spring. Named varieties by cuttings taken in late spring or autumn, or by grafting in spring.

Season of interest	Winter	Spring	Late spring	Summer	Late summer	Autumn
In full leaf	X—					—X
Autumn colour						
Flowers						
Fruits						
Bark and stem	X—					—X

The following five characteristics determine to a great extent the amount of attention a specific tree requires.

	When planted	5 years	20 years
Height	450 mm	1·0 m	3·5 m
Width	250 mm	450mm	2·0 m
Root spread	250 mm	600mm	2·5 m
Hardiness	C	C	B/C
Wind-firm	3	2	2

Plant care profile

	Minimum Average High
Site needs	X———X
Soil needs	X———X
Pruning	X
Staking	X———X
Maintenance	X———X

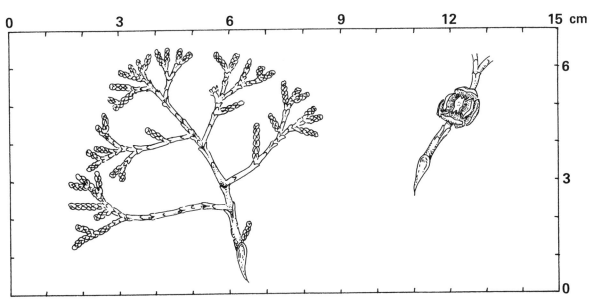

Chamaecyparis pisifera – CUPRESSACEAE
Sawara Cypress

A moderately hardy tree or shrub.
Origin Japan.

Uses
The Sawara Cypress and its taller varieties make fine specimen trees for large or medium gardens. The dwarf kinds are excellent in mixed plantings in small gardens or rock gardens.

Description
Dimensions Average ultimate size 9–10.5m (30–35ft) high by 4.5m (15ft) wide.
Rate of growth Moderate to slow.
Life span These conifers usually start to decline after 40–50 years, but moist conditions prolong their lives.
Habit Broadly pyramidal.
Leaves Mid- to dark green, with lighter reverse. The foliage is ferny in texture.
Flowers Inconspicuous.
Fruits Cones which turn brown when ripe, and are usually about the size of peas.
Bark On older conifers usually ridged and light brown. Pale to mid-brown, lightly ridged when young.

Features
Pleasing feathery foliage effect when young, tending to untidyness at the base when old. Sensitive to cold winds.
Pollution Tolerant.
Non-poisonous.

Varieties
Chamaecyparis pisifera 'Boulevard'. Average ultimate height 4–4.5m (13–15ft). Foliage variegated, blue, green, white or silver.
Chamaecyparis pisifera 'Filifera'. Average ultimate height 5–6m (17–20ft) by 4.5m (15ft). Foliage thin, thread-like and greyish green.
Chamaecyparis pisifera 'Filifera Aurea'. Similar to *C.p.* 'Filifera', but with golden foliage and slightly less vigorous – often only a bush.
Chamaecyparis pisifera 'Nana'. A fine dwarf conifer, ball-shaped and approximately 450mm (1½ft) high at maturity. Foliage usually bright green.
Chamaecyparis pisifera 'Plumosa Aurea'. Average ultimate height 7.5m (25ft). Foliage golden yellow and feathery.

Chamaecyparis pisifera 'Squarrosa Sulphurea'. A pleasing small tree or bush, slightly smaller than *C.p.* 'Plumosa Aurea'. Sulphur yellow foliage.

Requirements
Position A sheltered situation in an area with a moist, warm or mild temperate climate favours long-lived, well shaped trees. A site in full sun will improve the colour of blue and gold varieties, but all can tolerate light shade.
Soil A deep, well drained but moist loam that is slightly acid, pH about 6.5, is most suitable. Avoid shallow, hot, dry ground over chalk. On poor soils apply a dressing of 70g per sq. m (2 oz. per sq. yd) of general fertilizer before planting, and repeat each spring for the first few years.

Notes on culture
Planting Plant small conifers, preferably not more than 450mm (1½ft) high, in autumn or late spring. Staking and tying is not necessary for small plants. Keep the ground weed-free and mulched within a 450mm (1½ft) radius of young plants.

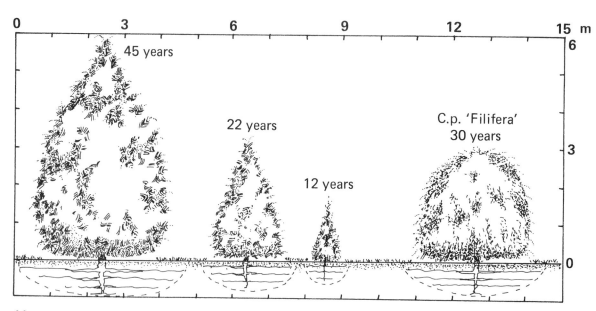

Space Allow each tree or shrub a minimum area of a diameter equal to its width at maturity and a similar distance from buildings.

Pruning Where single-stem trees are wanted prune to limit main shoots to one central leader. Cut back any damaged, diseased or untidy shoots to maintain a good shape, and if foliage is thin or sparse trim the shoots to induce branching and thickening of the foliage. All pruning should be done in late spring.

Plant associations Effective when planted around with ground cover such as Hypericums and with bulbs such as Narcissi. The dwarf varieties may be planted among other small conifers, or with rock plants or heathers.

Pest and disease control Rarely necessary.

Propagation By seed sown in spring. Named varieties by cuttings taken in spring or autumn, or by grafting in spring.

Season of interest	Winter	Spring	Late spring	Summer	Late summer	Autumn
In full leaf	X					X
Autumn colour						
Flowers						
Fruits						
Bark and stem						

The following five characteristics determine to a great extent the amount of attention a specific tree requires.

	When planted	5 years	20 years
Height	450 mm	900 mm	3·0 m
Width	250 mm	400 mm	1·5 m
Root spread	250 mm	500 mm	2·0 m
Hardiness	C	C	B/C
Wind-firm	3	2	2

Plant care profile

	Minimum Average High
Site needs	X——X
Soil needs	X
Pruning	X
Staking	X——X
Maintenance	X——X

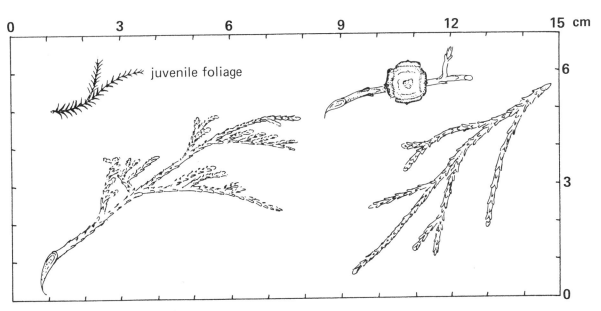

juvenile foliage

67

Chamaecyparis thyoides – CUPRESSACEAE
White Cypress

A moderately hardy evergreen tree.
Origin   North-eastern USA.

Uses
The White Cypress and its tall
varieties are excellent when used as
specimen trees. Dwarf kinds are
suitable for use in groups or in
mixed plantings in small gardens
and rock gardens.

Description
Dimensions   Average ultimate size
in gardens 7.5m (25ft) high by 3m
(10ft) wide.
Rate of growth   Moderate to slow.
Life span   Trees do not start to
decline until they are at least 50–60
years old.
Habit   Columnar or narrowly
pyramidal.
Leaves   Scale-like, dark green in
summer becoming bronze or
purplish green shades in winter.
Flowers   Inconspicuous.
Fruits   Round bluish grey cones,
about 6mm (¼ in.) in diameter.
Bark   On older trees, reddish
brown. Light to mid-brown when
young.

Features
The habit of the type is rather
more variable than the named
varieties. The species is less widely
planted than formerly, having been
superseded by some of the newer
and improved varieties and
selections. There is more risk of
leaf-scorch from strong freezing
winds, or during hard winters, than
with some other kinds of
Chamaecyparis.
Pollution   Moderately tolerant.
Non-poisonous.

Varieties
Chamaecyparis thyoides
'Andelyensis'. A narrow, erect
form, rarely more than 5m (17ft)
high. Green summer foliage,
turning bronze in winter.
Chamaecyparis thyoides
'Andelyensis Nana'. A compact,
round bush, not more than about
1.5m (5ft) high. Green foliage.
Chamaecyparis thyoides
'Ericoides'. A slow-growing plant
not more than about 1.2m (4ft)
high by the same wide. Foliage
feathery and juvenile, green in
summer, turning purple in winter.
Chamaecyparis thyoides   'Glauca'.
Grey-blue foliage.

Requirements
Position   As the White Cypress is
only moderately hardy, sunny but
sheltered situation in a moist warm
or mild temperate climate will
produce the best results. Protection
from cold and freezing winds is
highly desirable. These trees will
tolerate light shade.
Soil   Athough it naturally occurs in
cold, swampy ground, this Cypress
grows best in deep, well drained
but moist, medium to heavy loams
that are slightly acid, pH around
6.5. Avoid shallow chalk soils. On
poor soils apply a dressing of 70g
per sq. m (2oz. per sq. yd) of
general fertilizer before planting,
and repeat each spring for the first
few years.

Notes on culture
Planting   Plant in autumn or late
spring. Large trees can be moved,
but small plants become established
more rapidly. Staking and tying is
not necessary for small plants, but
trees over 900mm (3ft) high need
support until firmly rooted. Keep
the ground weed-free and mulched
within a 450mm (1½ft) radius of
young plants.

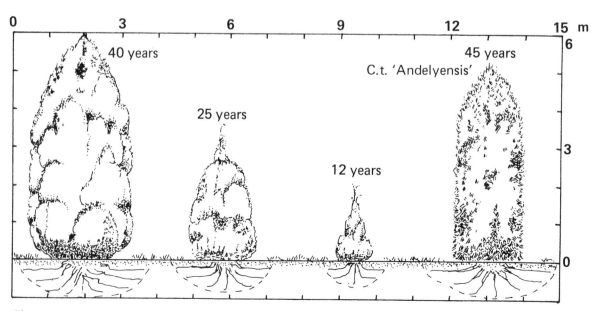

Space   Allow the true White Cypress and tall varieties a minimum area of 3m (10ft) diameter at maturity, and avoid planting closer to buildings than 6m (20ft). Dwarf varieties need proportionately less space.

Pruning   Prune to limit main shoots to one central leader. Cut back any damaged, diseased or untidy shoots to maintain a good shape, and if growth is thin or sparse trim the shoots lightly to induce branching and thickening of foliage. All pruning should be done in spring.

Plant associations   Dwarf and tall varieties look well among other dwarf conifers, or with heathers or rock plants.

Pest and disease control   Rarely necessary, but occasionally honey fungus attacks these trees. If planting on land which may have been contaminated, first remove all old tree stumps and sterilize the soil with formaldehyde. Allow four to six weeks for the formaldehyde fumes to dissipate from the soil before planting.

Propagation   By seed sown in spring. Named varieties by cuttings taken in autumn or spring, or by grafting in spring.

Season of interest	Winter	Spring	Late spring	Summer	Late summer	Autumn
In full leaf	X—					—X
Autumn colour		X—				X—
Flowers						
Fruits						
Bark and stem						

The following five characteristics determine to a great extent the amount of attention a specific tree requires.

	When planted	5 years	20 years
Height	450 mm	800 mm	3·0 m
Width	150 mm	350 mm	1·5 m
Root spread	200 mm	450 mm	2·0 m
Hardiness	C	B/C	B/C
Wind-firm	3	2	1

Plant care profile

	Minimum	Average	High
Site needs		X—	—X
Soil needs		X—	—X
Pruning		X	
Staking	X—	—X	
Maintenance	X		

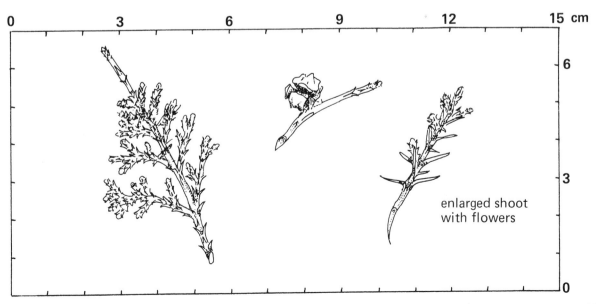

enlarged shoot with flowers

Cryptomeria japonica – TAXODIACEAE

Japanese Cedar

A moderately hardy evergreen tree.
Origin China and Japan.

Uses
The true Japanese Cedar is a fine specimen tree for the large or medium garden. The smaller varieties can make handsome specimens in more confined spaces, and are also suitable for planting among mixed conifers or in rock gardens.

Description
Dimensions Ultimate size can exceed 15m (50ft) high by 5m (17ft) wide.
Rate of growth Moderate to rapid.
Life span The species can be expected to live for 50 years or more, but the varieties often start to decline from half that age onwards.
Habit Variable, but usually pyramidal with spreading basal branches.
Leaves Green needles. The over-all effect of the foliage is light green in summer, becoming darker in winter.
Flowers Inconspicuous.
Fruits Rounded cones, brown when ripe, and about 12mm (½in.) across.

Bark On older conifers reddish brown, and peeling off in strips. The bark is similar on young plants but is less inclined to peel.

Features
The type Japanese Cedar makes a fine tree and is wind- and root-firm, but it is now less widely planted than varieties which have originated from it. Needs moist, but not waterlogged ground.
Pollution Fairly tolerant.
Non-poisonous.

Varieties
Cryptomeria japonica 'Elegans'. Ultimate size about 4–5m (13–17ft) high by 2.5–3m (8–10ft) wide. Foliage of the juvenile leaf type and blue-green in summer, purplish red in winter.
Cryptomeria japonica 'Globosa Nana'. A dwarf conifer which eventually reaches about 1m (3½ft) high by 1.5m (5ft) wide. Globose habit, green and pendulous foliage.
Cryptomeria japonica 'Lobbii 'Nana'. A form with a spreading rounded habit. Ultimate height about 1.8–2m (6–7ft) high by 2.5–3m (8–10ft) wide. Foliage stiffly pendulous, green in summer, becoming bronze-green in winter.

Cryptomeria japonica 'Vilmoriniana'. A slow-growing, rounded plant which reaches an ultimate size of about 1m (3½ft) high by 750mm (2½ft) wide. Foliage green in summer, bronze in winter.

Requirements
Position The finest specimens usually occur in areas with a warm or mild temperate climate and high rainfall. A sunny but sheltered site, well shielded from cold or drying winds, is best. Light shade is tolerated, but growth can be slow.
Soil A deep, well drained but moist loam, that is slightly acid, pH 6–6.5, is close to the ideal. On poor soils apply a dressing of 100g per sq. m (3oz. per sq. yd) of general fertilizer before planting, and repeat each spring for the first few years.

Notes on culture
Planting Plant small conifers, preferably not more than 600mm (2ft) high, in autumn or late spring. Staking and tying is not necessary for small plants, but those over 900mm (3ft) high need support until firmly rooted.

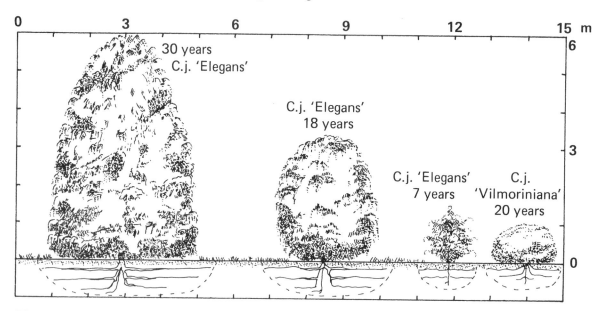

Space Allow the true Japanese Cedar a minimum area of 5m (17ft) diameter at maturity, and avoid planting closer to buildings than 7.5m (25ft). Smaller varieties need proportionately less space.

Pruning Prune tree forms to limit main shoots to one central leader, where tall specimens are wanted, until the required height is reached. Dwarf forms need an occasional trim to shorten untidy shoots and keep plants in good shape. All pruning should be done in late spring.

Plant associations The tree looks well with azaleas and rhododendrons. The smaller varieties may be planted among other conifers, or with heathers.

Pest and disease control Rarely necessary.

Propagation By seed sown in spring. Named varieties by cuttings taken in late summer.

Season of interest	Winter	Spring	Late spring	Summer	Late summer	Autumn
In full leaf		X—————————————————————				—X
Autumn colour		—X				X——
Flowers						
Fruits	——X				X——	
Bark and stem	X————————————————————————————					—X

The following five characteristics determine to a great extent the amount of attention a specific tree requires.

	When planted	5 years	20 years
Height	600 mm	1·2 m	3·5 m
Width	400 mm	750 mm	2·5 m
Root spread	500 mm	1·0 m	3·5 m
Hardiness	C	C	C
Wind-firm	3	2/3	2

Plant care profile

	Minimum Average High
Site needs	X————X
Soil needs	X————X
Pruning	X————X
Staking	X————X
Maintenance	X

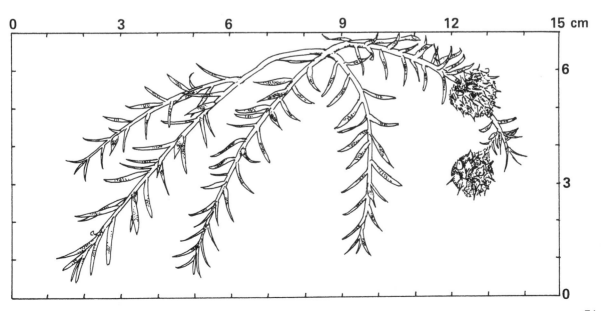

71

x Cupressocyparis leylandii – CUPRESSACEAE
Leyland Cypress

A hybrid between *Chamaecyparis nootkatensis* and *Cupressus macrocarpa*. A hardy evergreen tree.
Origin   Europe.

Uses
The Leyland Cypress is quite a versatile tree. It makes a good specimen for the larger garden, and it can also be planted in groups, or used for screening or shelter belts either inland or near the coast. Also widely planted for hedging, but can be too vigorous in small gardens.

Description
Dimensions   Average ultimate size 15–16.5m (50–55ft) high by 5–6m (17–20ft) wide, which is exceeded under good conditions.
Rate of growth   Moderate to rapid.
Life span   Trees start to decline after about 40 years.
Habit   Pyramidal, tapering from base to top.
Leaves   Dark green in summer, becoming grey-green in winter.
Flowers   Usually inconspicuous.
Fruits   Cones which are brown when ripe, and 12–18mm (½–¾ in.) in diameter.
Bark   Not visible as a rule, being concealed by the dense foliage.

Features
The Leyland Cypress is root- and wind-firm, and usually well covered with foliage.It has no serious faults, provided it is planted out when small.
Pollution   Resistant.
Non-poisonous.

Varieties
x *Cupressocyparis leylandii* 'Castlewellan' Gold'. Similar to type, but has golden foliage.
x *Cupressocyparis leylandii* 'Green Spire'. Slightly narrower than the type, and with lighter green foliage.
x *Cupressocyparis leylandii* 'Haggerston Grey'. Grey-green foliage.
x *Cupressocyparis leylandii* 'Naylor's Blue'. Bluish green foliage.

Requirements
Position   A mild or cool temperate climate is suitable. The Leyland Cypress does best in a sunny situation, but will also grow satisfactorily in light shade. The varieties will tolerate shade, but produce the best colour and form in sunny sites.

Soil   A deep, fertile, well drained loam that is slightly acid, pH 6.5–7, is near the ideal, but these trees will tolerate alkaline soils. Trees on shallow soils are inclined to be unstable and top-heavy. On poor soils apply a dressing of 100g per sq. m (3oz. per sq. yd) of general fertilizer before planting, and repeat each spring for the first few years.

Notes on culture
Planting   Plant small trees, up to 600mm (2ft) high, in late spring. Larger trees can be successfully moved, but they are slower to become established and are less wind-firm later and, unlike small plants, they need staking and tying.
Space   Allow a minimum area of 5m (17ft) diameter at maturity, and, to prevent excessive shade and damage to foundations, avoid planting closer to dwellings than 7.5m (25ft). These distances can be reduced when the Leyland Cypress is grown for hedging purposes.

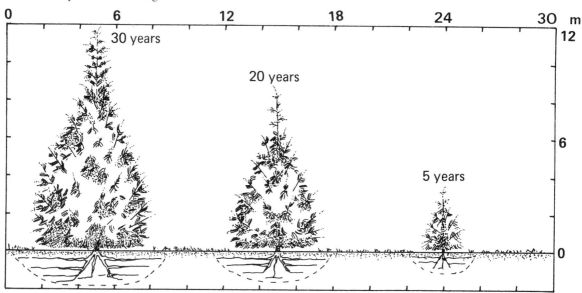

Here, heathers are interplanted with a ground-hugging Juniper and green fastigiate and gold conical conifers, providing ground cover and interest in summer, while the heathers are resting

A study of blue and gold, showing a blue Spruce with golden Cypress in late summer or autumn. These are seen to good effect in full sun

A late summer scene, in which *Juniperus conferta*, centre, provides a restful shade of light green. To the left is Ellwood's form of Lawson's Cypress. A blue *Cedrus atlantica glauca* forms part of the background

Blue Spruce can provide an almost startling effect in a garden, which is dominated by conifers as here, especially in weak winter sunshine

Pruning Prune to limit main shoots to one central leader, and cut back any damaged, diseased or untidy shoots to maintain a good shape. All pruning should be done in early autumn.
Plant associations Excellent with conifers or broad-leaved trees and shrubs as well as garden flowers.
Pest and disease control Rarely necessary.
Propagation By cuttings taken in late summer or early autumn.

Season of interest	Winter	Spring	Late spring	Summer	Late summer	Autumn
In full leaf	X					X
Autumn colour						
Flowers						
Fruits						
Bark and stem		X			X	

The following five characteristics determine to a great extent the amount of attention a specific tree requires.

	When planted	5 years	20 years
Height	600mm	3·0m	9·0m
Width	300mm	1·5m	4·0m
Root spread	300mm	2·5m	5·0m
Hardiness	B	B	A/B
Wind-firm	3	2	1

Plant care profile

	Minimum Average High
Site needs	X
Soil needs	X
Pruning	X——X
Staking	X——X
Maintenance	X

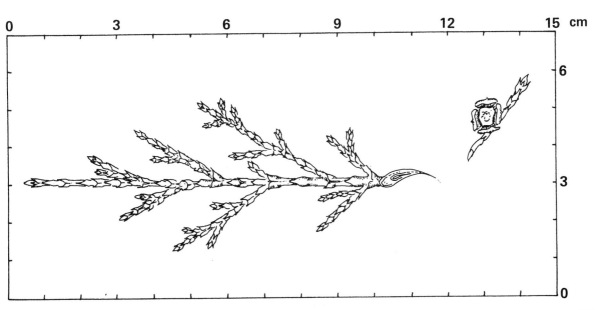

Cupressus glabra – CUPRESSACEAE
Arizona Cypress

A moderately hardy evergreen tree.
Origin Arizona.

Uses
This Cypress and its varieties make handsome specimen trees for the large or medium garden. They are especially effective when planted in grass.

Description
Dimensions Average ultimate size 9–10.5m (30–35ft) high by 3.5–4.5m (12–15ft) wide.
Rate of growth Moderate to slow.
Life span Trees start to decline after 50–60 years.
Habit Narrowly pyramidal, becoming more columnar with age. The branch arrangement is circular and plume-like.
Leaves Small scales. The general effect of the foliage is a greyish blue green.
Flowers The male flowers at the shoot tips are yellow with pollen in spring, but the female flowers are inconspicuous.
Fruits Purple-brown cones, about 18–25mm (¾-1in.) across at maturity.
Bark Fairly smooth and purple, flaking to expose yellow patches.

Features
This is one of the hardiest of the true Cypresses, and under congenial conditions it makes a wind-firm tree.
Pollution Fairly tolerant.
Non-poisonous.

Variety
Cupressus glabra 'Pyramidalis' *(C. arizonica* 'Conica'). Makes a very pleasing narrow pyramid of feathery bluish green foliage.

Requirements
Position This Cypress needs a warm or mild temperate climate, and a sunny but sheltered site, well protected from harsh cold winds and severe frost, is most suitable.
Soil A well drained, medium loam that is slightly acid to neutral, pH 6.5–7, produces the best results.

Notes on culture
Planting Plant small trees, 450–600mm (1½–2ft) high, in autumn or late spring. Container-grown plants should be used, as this Cypress tends to grow tap roots, which makes transplanting difficult. Staking and tying is not normally necessary for small plants, but those over 900mm (3ft) high need support until firmly rooted. Keep the ground around young plants weed-free, well watered and mulched.
Space Allow a minimum area of 4.5m (15ft) diameter at maturity, and avoid planting closer to buildings than 6m (20ft).
Pruning Prune to limit main shoots to one central leader. This should be done in spring. No further pruning is usually necessary.
Plant associations This tree is effective with red or blue foliage plants for contrast.

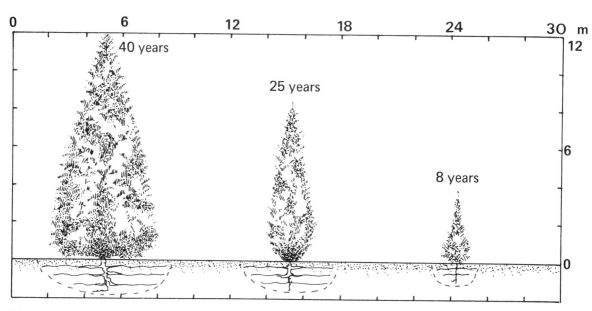

Pest and disease control Aphids, which can weaken trees by feeding on the sap, causing bronzing and premature leaf fall, can be controlled by malathion or other insecticide sprays. Red spider mites can also impair tree health by their feeding activities, causing bronzing and covering the leaves with fine webbing; they can be controlled by derris, diazinon or dimethoate sprays. Seedlings sometimes suffer from damping off and grey mould, but clean growing conditions, adequate space and light and pre-sowing treatment of seeds with thiram fungicide are good preventive measures. Remove any severely infected plants and spray with benomyl or similar fungicide against grey mould.

Propagation By seed sown in spring. Named varieties by cuttings taken in late summer or autumn and by grafting in spring.

Season of interest	Winter	Spring	Late spring	Summer	Late summer	Autumn
In full leaf	X					X
Autumn colour						
Flowers						
Fruits		X			X	
Bark and stem	X					X

The following five characteristics determine to a great extent the amount of attention a specific tree requires.

	When planted	5 years	20 years
Height	600 mm	2·0 m	7·5 m
Width	200 mm	750 mm	2·5 m
Root spread	200 mm	1·0 m	3·5 m
Hardiness	C	C	B/C
Wind-firm	3	2	1

Plant care profile

	Minimum Average High
Site needs	X———X
Soil needs	X———X
Pruning	X———X
Staking	X———X
Maintenance	X———X

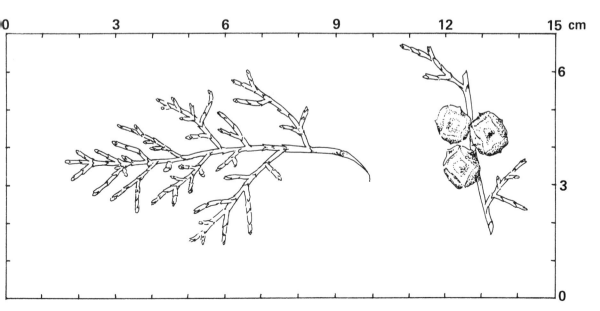

Ginkgo biloba – GINKGOACEAE
Maidenhair Tree

A moderately hardy deciduous tree.
Origin China.

Uses
The Maidenhair Tree can be very effectively used as a specimen tree in a large or medium garden.

Description
Dimensions Variable, but ultimate size can exceed 10.5m (35ft) high by 5–6m (17–20ft) wide in gardens.
Rate of growth Moderate to slow.
Life span Under good conditions trees will live for well over 100 years.
Habit Varies somewhat: male trees are broadly pyramidal in outline, female trees are often more spreading.
Leaves The unusual fan-shaped leaves are a major feature. They are light green and leathery, turning to warm shades of yellow and amber in autumn just before leaf fall.
Flowers The short yellow male catkins when present usually appear about the same time as the leaves open. The inconspicuous bract-like female flowers only develop after hot summers.

Fruits Greenish fruits, vaguely plum-shaped.
Bark Dark grey, and cracking as trees age.

Features
The Maidenhair Tree is of considerable botanical interest. It is thought to be prehistoric in origin, and the last of its kind. As a garden tree it requires little by way of attention, being root-firm and generally free of problems.
Pollution Moderately resistant.
Non-poisonous.

Varieties
Ginkgo biloba 'Fastigiata'. Columnar and upright in outline, and rather narrower than the species.
Ginkgo biloba 'Pendula'. Broader, more spreading, and pendulous in habit.

Requirements
Position A sunny but sheltered situation, preferably in a lowland area with a warm or mild temperate climate, is most suitable. Protection from cold and freezing winds is necessary.

Soil A deep, fertile, well drained loam, well supplied with organic matter and slightly acid to neutral, pH 6.7–7, is near the ideal.

Notes on culture
Planting Plant small trees, 600–900mm (2–3ft) high, in late spring. Staking and tying is not necessary for small plants, but larger trees need support until firmly rooted. Keep the ground weed-free, well watered and mulched within a 600mm (2ft) radius of young plants.
Space This tree requires room for development, so allow a minimum area of 4m (13ft) diameter at maturity. Temporary plantings that are removed as necessary in later years may be made closer to the young trees, which are initially slow-growing. Avoid planting closer to buildings than 7.5m (25ft).

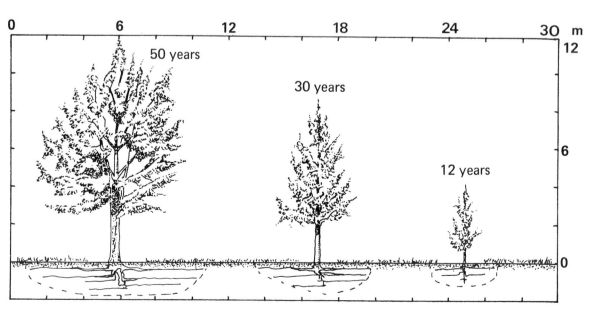

Pruning The Maidenhair Tree resents being pruned, often dying back from each cut. Prune to limit main shoots to one central leader until the required height is reached, removing any surplus shoots in spring. Thereafter keep pruning to a minimum, cutting out only diseased or untidy branches which seriously affect the well-being or shape of the tree.
Plant associations Looks well with berberis or planted around with ground cover or shrubs.
Pest and disease control Rarely necessary once plants are past the seedling stage. Sometimes affected by damping off, control by use of thiram seed dressing.
Propagation By imported seed sown as soon as ripe, during late summer or autumn.

Season of interest	Winter	Spring	Late spring	Summer	Late summer	Autumn
In full leaf			X————		————X	
Autumn colour					X——X	
Flowers			X——X			
Fruits						X——X
Bark and stem						

The following five characteristics determine to a great extent the amount of attention a specific tree requires.

	When planted	5 years	20 years
Height	900 mm	1·5 m	6·0 m
Width	450 mm	1·0 m	3·0 m
Root spread	450 mm	1·5 m	4·0 m
Hardiness	C	C	B
Wind-firm	3	2	2

Plant care profile

	Minimum Average High
Site needs	X————X
Soil needs	X
Pruning	X————X
Staking	X
Maintenance	X————X

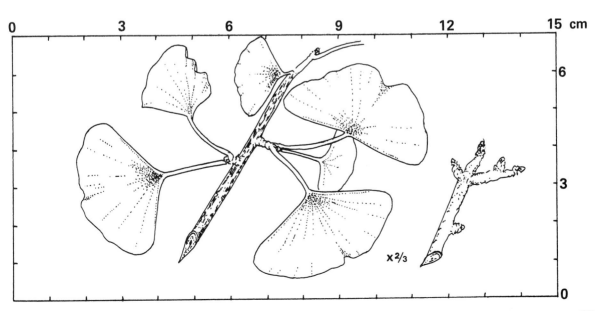

x²/₃

77

Juniperus chinensis – CUPRESSACEAE
Chinese Juniper

A hardy evergreen tree.
Origin China and Japan.

Uses
The Chinese Juniper and its varieties make good specimen trees on lawns, and they are also effective in mixed plantings.

Description
Dimensions Average ultimate size in gardens 6–7.5m (20–25ft) high by 1.5–2m (5–7ft) wide.
Rate of growth Usually slow.
Life span The Juniper can be expected to continue growing for 50–60 years or more before starting to decline.
Habit In early years usually narrowly pyramidal, later becoming columnar with a conical top half.
Leaves Needle-like; dark grey-green in the adult tree, but the juvenile foliage is bluish green.
Flowers Male and female flowers are often borne on different trees, but are comparatively insignificant.
Fruits Blue-black berries, which follow the female flowers.
Bark Brownish, inclined to be stringy.

Features
The Chinese Juniper requires little attention, is well rooted and wind-firm, and in general has most of the traits required in a good garden tree.
Pollution Tolerant.
Non-poisonous.

Varieties
Juniperus chinensis 'Aurea'. A most useful form, with golden yellow foliage. Slightly less vigorous than the type.
Juniperus chinensis 'Japonica'. A bush form rarely exceeding 1.5m (5ft) high. Densely branched and compact in habit, with prickly green juvenile foliage. This variety deserves to be more widely grown.
Juniperus chinensis 'Keteleeri'. Narrowly pyramidal in outline. Foliage usually adult, and of a brighter green than the type.
Juniperus chinensis 'Pyramidalis'. Of narrow, upright habit and slow-growing. Average ultimate height about 3m (10ft). Foliage an outstanding blue-green, and juvenile in form.

Requirements
Position A mild temperate climate suits these trees, and the best examples are usually found in open, sunny sites, protected from cold north and east winds.
Soil A well drained but moist loam that is slightly acid, pH 6.5, is most suitable. However, the Chinese Juniper can tolerate dry, alkaline, chalky soils better than most conifers.

Notes on culture
Planting Plant small conifers, 600–900mm (2–3ft) high. Late spring is the best time for planting, but if necessary plants can be moved in late summer or early autumn. Staking and tying is not necessary for small plants, but those over 900mm (3ft) high need support until firmly rooted.
Space Allow each tree or bush a minimum area equal in diameter to half its height at maturity, and double that distance from dwellings.
Pruning Cut back any damaged, diseased or untidy shoots to maintain a good shape. This should be done in late spring.

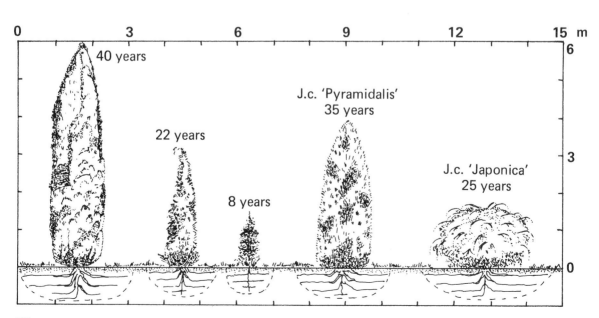

Plant associations These Junipers look well when planted in association with shrubs and heath plants.

Pest and disease control Conifer spinning mites, usually to be seen as small orange reddish mites, sometimes feed on and weaken plants; they can be checked by malathion sprays. Juniper scale, which appears as whitish encrustations on stems and leaves, weakening plants by feeding on them, can be controlled by malathion or diazinon sprays. The caterpillars of the Juniper webber moth, which devour the leaves and spin the shoots together with fine webbing, can be controlled by spraying or dusting with HCH. Rust diseases, caused by various organisms, appear as yellow or orange pustules on leaves; they can be controlled by spraying with a copper or thiram fungicide to prevent further spread.

Propagation By seed sown in late summer or autumn. Named varieties by cuttings taken in late summer or autumn.

Season of interest	Winter	Spring	Late spring	Summer	Late summer	Autumn
In full leaf	X————	————	————	————	————	———X
Autumn colour						
Flowers					X————|———X	
Fruits						
Bark and stem						

The following five characteristics determine to a great extent the amount of attention a specific tree requires.

	When planted	5 years	20 years
Height	900 mm	1·25 m	3·0 m
Width	300 mm	400 mm	1·0 m
Root spread	300 mm	450 mm	1·5 m
Hardiness	C	B/C	B
Wind-firm	3	2/3	1

Plant care profile

	Minimum	Average	High
Site needs		X	
Soil needs		X	
Pruning	X———	—X	
Staking	X———	—X	
Maintenance	X———	—X	

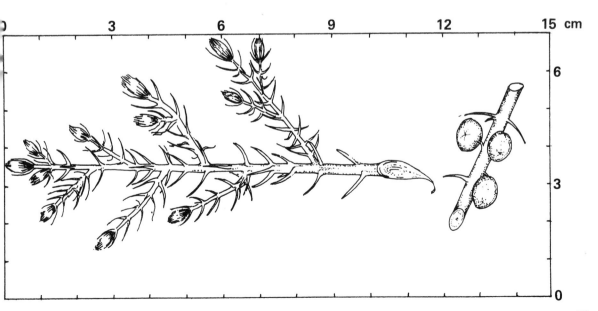

Juniperus communis – CUPRESSACEAE
Common Juniper

A hardy evergreen tree or shrub.
Origin Asia, Europe and USA.

Uses
The Common Juniper itself is not widely planted, but its varieties provide useful specimen trees for small as well as large gardens. The Irish Juniper is particularly useful in confined spaces, as are the dwarf forms, which are excellent planted in groups, in small gardens or rock gardens.

Description
Dimensions Variable, but average ultimate size rarely exceeds 4–5m (13–17ft) high by 1.5–2m (5–7ft) wide.
Rate of growth Usually slow, in exposed sites very slow.
Life span This Juniper can be expected to continue growing for at least 40 years before starting to decline.
Habit Variable, ranging from narrowly pyramidal to broadly spreading.
Leaves Prickly. The foliage, which is open and juvenile in texture, is grey-green.
Flowers Inconspicuous.

Fruits Berry-like fruits which take two seasons to ripen. They are green at first, turning blue or black, and have a covering of whitish bloom.
Bark Usually concealed beneath fairly dense foliage.

Features
The Common Juniper and its varieties are less demanding than many garden trees and shrubs as regards soil and cultivation, requiring a minimum of attention.
Pollution Moderately resistant.
Non-poisonous.

Varieties
Juniperus communis 'Compressa'. A gem among dwarf conifers. Ultimate size approximately 600–750mm (2–2½ft) high by 150–200mm (6–8in.) wide. Pleasing grey-green foliage which is retained all the year round.
Juniperus communis 'Depressa Aurea'. A low ground-cover plant which eventually reaches 2–3m (7–10ft) across. Foliage golden in summer, turning bronze in winter, and prickly to touch.

Juniperus communis 'Hibernica' (Irish Juniper). An upright, narrowly pyramidal form, rarely more than 3–4.5m (10–15ft) high by 750–900mm (2½–3ft) wide. Foliage green and prickly.
Juniperus communis 'Repanda'. A low-growing ground carpeter, ultimately reaching 2–3m (7–10ft) across. Foliage dull green in summer, becoming bronze in winter.

Requirements
Position A mild or cool temperate climate suits these trees. The Common Juniper prefers an open, sunny situation but can tolerate light shade. Golden forms need full sun for best results. The species can stand elevated, exposed sites, but shelter from strong prevailing winds maintains a better tree shape. *J.c.* 'Compressa' is best protected from strong and freezing winds.
Soil A well drained, medium loam that is neutral, pH 7, usually produces the best specimens. However, these Junipers can be grown successfully on dry, shallow chalk soils, as well as on acid, peaty ground.

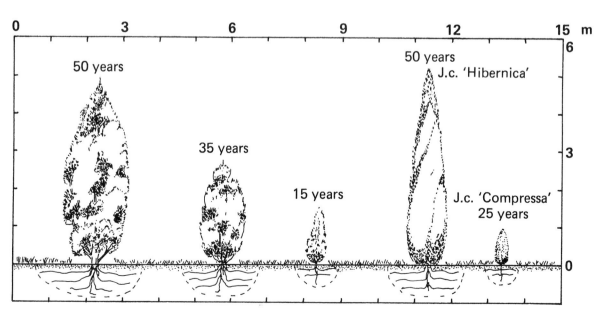

Notes on culture

Planting Plant small conifers, preferably not more than 900mm (3ft) high. Late spring is the best time for planting, but plants can also be successfully moved in late summer or early autumn. Staking and tying is not usually necessary for small plants, but those over 900mm (3ft) high need support until firmly rooted.

Space Allow a minimum 3m (10ft) diameter for plants at maturity and a similar distance from buildings. Although these are slow-growing plants, avoid overcrowding in the early years or lower foliage may be lost, exposing bare branches. The taller Common Junipers, including the Irish Juniper, are best not planted closer to buildings than 1.2–1.5m (4–5ft).

Pruning Cut back any damaged, diseased or untidy shoots to maintain a good shape. This should be done in late spring.

Plant associations This Juniper looks well with other dwarf conifers and in turf.

Pest and disease control Juniper scale, appearing as whitish encrustations on stems and leaves, can be controlled by malathion or diazinon sprays. Juniper webber moth caterpillars, which devour the leaves and spin the shoots together with fine webbing, can be controlled by HCH. Rusts, which occur as yellow or orange pustules on leaves, can be checked by spraying with a copper or thiram fungicide.

Propagation By seed sown in late summer or early autumn. Named varieties by cuttings taken in late summer or early autumn.

Season of interest	Winter	Spring	Late spring	Summer	Late summer	Autumn
In full leaf	X———					——X
Autumn colour						
Flowers						
Fruits					X——	
Bark and stem						

The following five characteristics determine to a great extent the amount of attention a specific tree requires.

	When planted	5 years	20 years
Height	750 mm	900 mm	2·0 m
Width	250 mm	300 mm	900mm
Root spread	250 mm	350 mm	1·2 m
Hardiness	B	A	A
Wind-firm	2	1/2	1

Plant care profile

	Minimum	Average	High
Site needs	X——	—X	
Soil needs			X
Pruning	X———	—X	
Staking	X		
Maintenance	X———	—X	

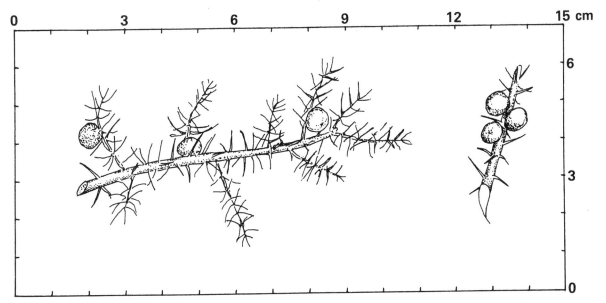

Juniperus conferta – CUPRESSACEAE
Shore Juniper

A moderately hardy evergreen shrub.
Origin Japan.

Uses
The Shore Juniper provides good ground cover among rocks or stones, on banks, or over retaining walls. As its name suggests, it is particularly suitable for planting in coastal districts.

Description
Dimensions The width, which is in this case more important than the height, can reach 3–4m (10–13ft).
Rate of growth Slow to moderate.
Life span Variable, but 30–40 years or even more is not uncommon. Experience of this plant is limited, as it was introduced into Western gardens only in this century.
Habit Prostrate and ground-hugging, sprawling over ground, banks and walls.
Leaves Sharp, prickly, and of a pleasant light to mid-green.
Flowers Inconspicuous
Fruits Round black berries, covered with greyish-white bloom.
Bark Insignificant, concealed by foliage.

Features
An excellent ground-cover shrub, forming a fairly dense mat. When established smothers weed seedlings.
Pollution Moderately tolerant.
Non-poisonous.

Varieties
At present no noteworthy varieties are available to amateur gardeners.

Requirements
Position A mild or warm temperate climate is needed. The Shore Juniper prefers an open, sunny situation but can tolerate light shade.Coastal situations protected from cold and freezing winds are most suitable.
Soil A well drained, light to medium loam that is neutral or nearly so, pH 6.8–7, seems to produce the best results.

Notes on culture
Planting Plant two- or three-year-old conifers in late summer, early autumn or late spring. Provided that plants can be mulched and watered if need be, those transplanted in spring tend to become established most rapidly. As with all procumbent plants, it is especially important to make sure the ground is clear of perennial weeds: if necessary defer planting. Keep the ground around young plants weed-free and mulched.
Space This Juniper should preferably be given room to ramble over rocks or low walls, and should not be hedged around with tall subjects. Allow a minimum area of 3m (10ft) diameter at maturity and half that distance from buildings. Temporary plantings may be made closer to the young shrubs, but filler plants must be removed in good time to prevent overcrowding. Close planting is necessary for quick soil cover.
Pruning Cut back any damaged, diseased or untidy shoots to maintain a good shape. This should be done in late spring.

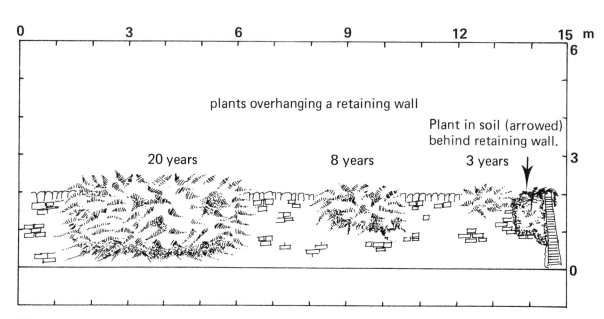

plants overhanging a retaining wall

Plant in soil (arrowed) behind retaining wall.

20 years   8 years   3 years

Plant associations The ground-hugging habit of this Juniper makes it a good contrast with upright dwarf conifers, and it also looks attractive among heathers, its different foliage texture adding interest.

Pest and disease control Juniper scale, appearing as whitish encrustations on stems and leaves, can be controlled by malathion or diazinon sprays. Juniper webber moth caterpillars, which devour the leaves and spin the shoots together with fine webbing, can be controlled by HCH. Rusts, which occur as yellow or orange pustules on leaves, can be checked by spraying with a copper or thiram fungicide.

Propagation By cuttings taken in late summer and early autumn. Seed is rarely used, as this conifer only infrequently sets seed in cultivation.

Season of interest	Winter	Spring	Late spring	Summer	Late summer	Autumn
In full leaf	X———					———X
Autumn colour						
Flowers						
Fruits						
Bark and stem						

The following five characteristics determine to a great extent the amount of attention a specific tree requires.

	When planted	5 years	20 years
Height	100 mm	200 mm	300 mm
Width	200 mm	1·2 m	4·0 m
Root spread	150 mm	1·2 m	5·0 m
Hardiness	C	C	B/C
Wind-firm	2	1	1

Plant care profile

	Minimum Average High
Site needs	X
Soil needs	X
Pruning	X———X
Staking	X
Maintenance	X———X

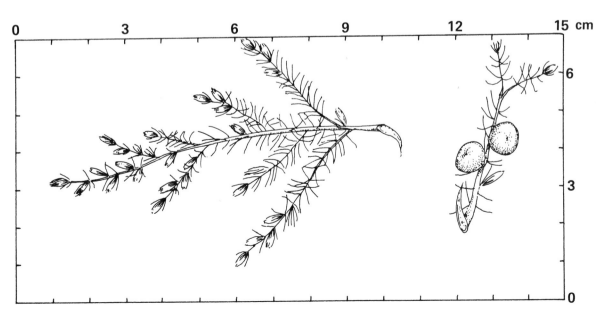

Juniperus horizontalis – CUPRESSACEAE
Creeping Juniper

A very hardy procumbent shrub.
Origin North-eastern USA.

Uses
The Creeping Juniper and its varieties provide first-class ground cover on level or sloping ground, over banks or cascading over low retaining walls.

Description
Dimensions Average ultimate size 300–380mm (1–1¼ft) high by 1.5–4.5m (5–15ft) wide.
Rate of growth Slow to moderate.
Life span Variable, but 30 years or more is not uncommon.
Habit As its name indicates, this plant is ground-hugging and procumbent, forming a carpet of foliage.
Leaves Blue-green, and juvenile in form. The tips of the foliage are whip-like.
Flowers None in cultivation.
Fruits Not produced by the Creeping Juniper or its varieties.
Bark Inconspicuous among the mat of shoots and growth.

Features
This Juniper makes up for its lack of seeds by its ability to form roots along the length of the stems, which ensures a ready means of natural increase. However, this tendency to spread does not as a rule cause any great problem in gardens.
Pollution Tolerant.
Non-poisonous.

Varieties
Juniperus horizontalis 'Bar Harbour'. Foliage blue-green, mat-forming type with whip-like tips.
Juniperus horizontalis 'Douglasii'. Foliage consists of both adult and juvenile types, and is blue-green in summer and purple in winter.
Juniperus horizontalis 'Glauca'. A prostrate form, with shoots flat and mat-forming. Grey-blue foliage with whip-like tips.
Juniperus horizontalis 'Montana'. Ultimately about 3m (10ft) diameter. Feathery, silvery blue foliage.

Juniperus horizontalis 'Plumosa' (Andorra Juniper). Ultimately about 400–450mm (16–18in.) high by 2–3m (7–10ft) wide. Grey-green summer foliage, turning purplish in winter.
Juniperus horizontalis 'Wiltonii'. Similar in habit to *J.h.* 'Glauca', but with less blue, more silvery foliage.

Requirements
Position A cool or mild temperate climate suits these conifers. The Creeping Juniper and especially its coloured varieties grow best in sunny situations that are sheltered from cold and freezing winds. Although this Juniper is very hardy and likely to survive harsh conditions, foliage scorched by wind takes time to recover.
Soil A well drained, light to medium loam that is slightly acid, pH around 6.5, is close to the ideal. Unlike some of the other Junipers, this conifer does not occur naturally on or over chalk or limestone.

Notes on culture
Planting Ideally plant young conifers. Late spring is the best time for planting, but plants can also be successfully moved in late summer or early autumn. Keep the

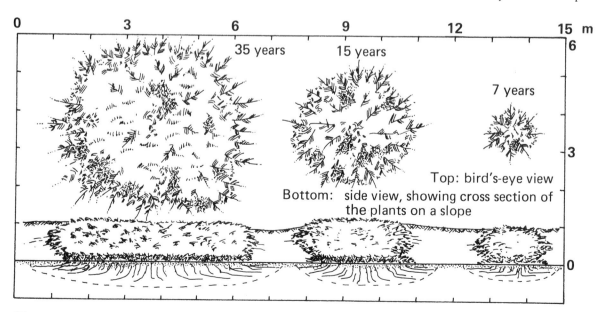

Top: bird's-eye view
Bottom: side view, showing cross section of the plants on a slope

35 years   15 years   7 years

around young plants weed-free and well mulched.

Space Allow a minimum area of 3–4m (10–13ft) diameter at maturity or one-third that distance from buildings, unless plants are to be contained by clipping. As with other mat-forming Junipers, this conifer produces a good carpet effect when allowed to develop unimpeded by tall plants or obstructions.

Pruning The less cutting the better, apart from trimming damaged or untidy shoots. However, where the foliage is thin or sparse cutting back new shoots by a third to half in spring will encourage new growth and thickening.

Plant associations The Creeping Juniper and its varieties provide a contrast of habit and interest when planted with upright conifers.

Pest and disease control Given adequate space and good cultivation, the Creeping Juniper and its varieties are usually fairly free from ailments. Juniper scale, which occasionally appears as whitish encrustations on stems and leaves, can be controlled by malathion or diazinon sprays. Juniper webber moth caterpillars,

which devour the leaves and spin the shoots together with fine webbing, can be controlled by HCH. Rusts, which may occur as yellow or orange pustules on leaves, can be checked by spraying with a copper or thiram fungicide.

Propagation By cuttings taken in early summer or late autumn. Select material from plants having the best colour and characteristics.

Season of interest	Winter	Spring	Late spring	Summer	Late summer	Autumn
In full leaf	X					X
Autumn colour						
Flowers						
Fruits						
Bark and stem						

The following five characteristics determine to a great extent the amount of attention a specific tree requires.

	When planted	5 years	20 years
Height	100 mm	150 mm	200 mm
Width	250 mm	1·0 m	3·5 m
Root spread	200 mm	1·0 m	3·5 m
Hardiness	B	A	A
Wind-firm	2	1	1

Plant care profile

	Minimum	Average	High
Site needs		X	
Soil needs		X	
Pruning	X	X	
Staking	X		
Maintenance	X	X	

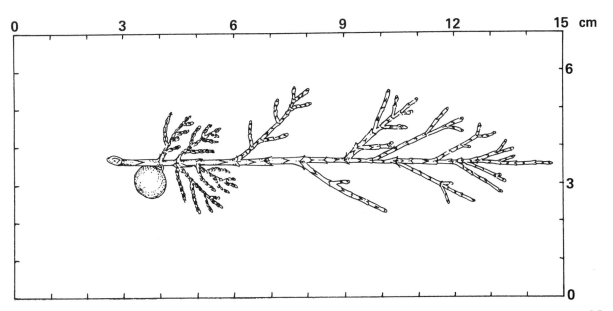

Juniperus x media – CUPRESSACEAE
Hybrid Juniper, Media Juniper

A naturally occurring hybrid with characteristics of *J. chinensis* and *J. sabina*. A hardy evergreen tree or shrub.
Origin Asia.

Uses
The Hybrid Juniper and its varieties can be used for ground cover as individual specimens and in groups of plants, as well as on banks and in rock gardens.

Description
Dimensions Variable, as with many hybrids, but ultimate size up to 2.5m (8ft) high by 3–4m (10–13ft) wide.
Rate of growth Ranges from slow to rapid.
Life span This Juniper can be expected to continue growing for 30 years or more before starting to decline.
Habit Very distinctive: bushy, broadening out into an inverted cone with a flat or saucer-shaped top.
Leaves Scale-like, varying shades of green, sometimes prickly. The foliage consists of varying proportions of both adult and juvenile forms, with some older plants taking on all adult form.

Flowers Inconspicuous.
Fruits Berries are formed but infrequently borne.
Bark Not very conspicuous, being hidden by fairly dense foliage.

Features
The Hybrid Juniper and its varieties make good garden subjects, needing only a minimum of attention. Accommodating in its preferences of soil and situation.
Pollution Tolerant.
Non-poisonous.

Varieties
Juniperus x *media* 'Blaauw'. Ultimate height and width, 2–2.5m (7–8ft). The main branches rise at a sharp angle from the ground, forming an inverted cone of bluish grey-green foliage with a hollow centre.
Juniperus x *media* 'Hetzii'. More vigorous than *J.* x *m.* 'Blaauw', ultimately reaching 2.5–3m (8–10ft) high by 3–3.5m (10–12ft) wide. Foliage a light grey-green.
Juniperus x *media* 'Old Gold'. Forms a compact mass of gold foliage, retaining its colour well through the year. Ultimate size approximately 2m (7ft) high by 2.5m (8ft) wide.

Juniperus x *media* 'Pfitzerana Aurea'. A good gold form which stands clipping. Ultimate size 1–1.5m (3½–5ft) high by 3–4m (10–13ft) wide.
Juniperus x *media* 'Plumosa Aurea'. A moderately slow-growing form which eventually reaches 3m (10ft) high by 3–3.5m (10–12ft) wide in good conditions. Foliage mostly of the adult type, yellowish green in summer, turning bronze-gold in winter.

Requirements
Position A mild or warm temperate climate is suitable, and open, sunny situations protected from cold and freezing winds produce the best results.
Soil A well drained, light to medium loam that is slightly acid to neutral, pH 6.5–7, is ideal. However, this Juniper can tolerate and grow on dry chalk or limestone soils without serious harm. On poor soils apply a dressing of 70g per sq. m (2oz. per sq. yd) of general fertilizer before planting, and repeat each spring for the first few years.

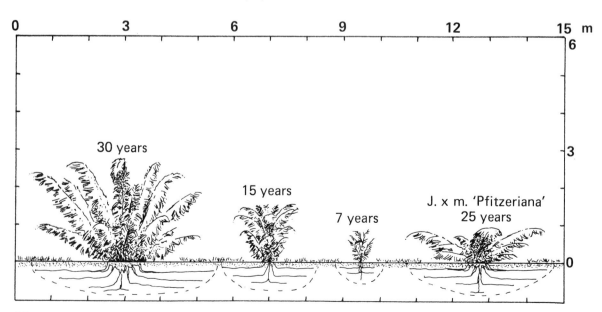

Notes on culture

Planting Plant small conifers, 300–450mm (1–1½ft) high. Late spring is the best time for planting, but plants can also be successfully moved in late summer or early autumn. Staking and tying is not usually necessary. Keep the ground around young plants weed-free, well watered and mulched.

Space Allow each tree or shrub a minimum area equal in diameter to its width at maturity and half to two-thirds that distance from buildings.

Pruning Cut back any damaged, diseased or untidy shoots to maintain a good shape. This should be done in late spring.

Plant associations Effective when planted around with flowering bulbs.

Pest and disease control The Hybrid Juniper and its varieties are usually fairly free from ailments. Juniper scale, which occasionally appears as whitish encrustations on stems and leaves, can be controlled by malathion or diazinon sprays. Juniper webber moth caterpillars, which devour the leaves and spin the shoots together with fine webbing, can be controlled by HCH. Rusts, which may occur as yellow or orange pustules on leaves, can be checked by spraying with a copper or thiram fungicide.

Propagation By cuttings taken in late summer or autumn.

Season of interest	Winter	Spring	Late spring	Summer	Late summer	Autumn
In full leaf	X————					————X
Autumn colour						
Flowers						
Fruits						
Bark and stem						

The following five characteristics determine to a great extent the amount of attention a specific tree requires.

	When planted	5 years	20 years
Height	450mm	750mm	2·0m
Width	300mm	600mm	1·5m
Root spread	300mm	750mm	2·0m
Hardiness	C	B/C	B
Wind-firm	2	1	1

Plant care profile

	Minimum	Average	High
Site needs		X	
Soil needs		X	
Pruning	X————	————X	
Staking	X		
Maintenance	X————	————X	

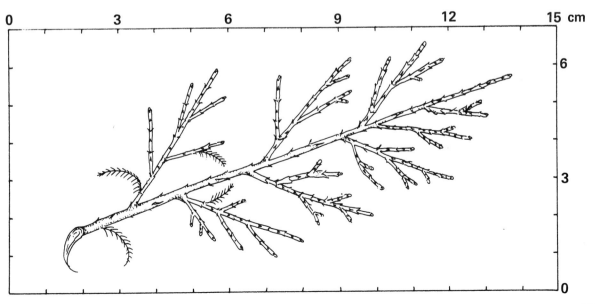

Juniperus procumbens – CUPRESSACEAE
Procumbent Juniper, Japanese Creeping Juniper

A moderately hardy evergreen shrub.
Origin Japan.

Uses
The Procumbent Juniper is an excellent ground-cover plant: it can be set among stones or rocks, on banks and slopes, or allowed to flow over retaining walls.

Description
Dimensions Ultimate size up to 300–450mm (1–1½ft) high by 3–5m (10–17ft) wide.
Rate of growth Slow to moderate.
Life span Plants can be expected to live for 30 years and upwards.
Habit As its name implies, this Juniper is prostrate and spreading, keeping close to the ground. It differs from the Shore Juniper in that the growths tend to be inclined upwards.
Leaves Sharply pointed, up to 8mm (⅓in.) long, and glaucous green on the upper surface with bright green reverse. The foliage of *J. procumbens* is harder and more prickly than that of *J. squamata*, to which it resembles.
Flowers Unusually borne in cultivation.

Fruits In the wild state the Procumbent Juniper produces blue, or black, bloom covered berries, but these rarely if ever appear on garden plants.
Bark This is rarely seen, being hidden by the close-knit foliage.

Features
This is essentially an attractive ground-hugging, mat-forming plant.
Pollution Moderately tolerant.
Non-poisonous.

Variety
Juniperus procumbens 'Nana'. More ground-hugging and less vigorous than the type. Retains its bright green foliage colour well throughout the year. This variety is superior to and more widely planted than the species.

Requirements
Position A sunny but sheltered situation in an area with a mild temperate climate suits these Junipers best. In shaded sites the foliage tends to be thin and sparse.
Soil A well drained, light to medium loam that is neutral, pH 7 or near, produces good results.

Notes on culture
Planting Plant small conifers. Late spring is the best time for planting, but plants can also be successfully moved in late summer or early autumn. Make sure the ground is clear of perennial weeds: if necessary defer planting. Keep the ground around young plants weed-free, well watered and mulched.
Space This Juniper is vigorous and wide-spreading, so give it adequate room to develop. Allow a minimum area of 4m (13ft) diameter at maturity and one-third that distance from buildings. Temporary plantings may be made closer to young Junipers, but filler plants must be removed in good time to prevent overcrowding.
Pruning Cut back any damaged, diseased or untidy shoots, and give an occasional trim as necessary to contain or shape plants. All pruning should be done in late spring.
Plant associations The Procumbent Juniper provides a useful contrast when planted in association with upright conifers, or with plants such as heathers.

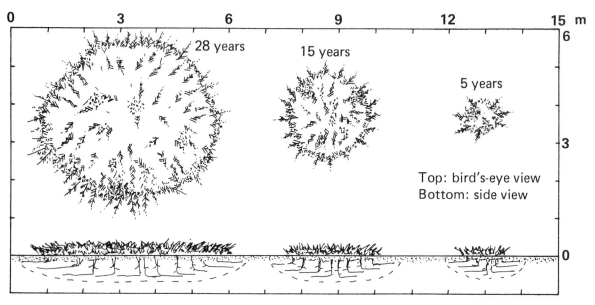

28 years   15 years   5 years

Top: bird's-eye view
Bottom: side view

Pest and disease control Juniper scale, appearing as whitish encrustations on stems and leaves, can be controlled by malathion or diazinon sprays. Juniper webber moth caterpillars, which devour the leaves and spin the shoots together with fine webbing, can be controlled by HCH. Rusts, which occur as yellow or orange pustules on leaves, can be checked by spraying with a copper or thiram fungicide.

Propagation By cuttings taken in late summer or early autumn. Seed is not set by cultivated plants.

Season of interest	Winter	Spring	Late spring	Summer	Late summer	Autumn
In full leaf	X————					————X
Autumn colour						
Flowers						
Fruits						
Bark and stem						

The following five characteristics determine to a great extent the amount of attention a specific tree requires.

	When planted	5 years	20 years
Height	100 mm	125 mm	150 mm
Width	200 mm	1·0 m	3·5 m
Root spread	200 mm	1·2 m	4·0 m
Hardiness	C	B/C	B/C
Wind-firm	2	2	1

Plant care profile

	Minimum Average High
Site needs	X————X
Soil needs	X
Pruning	X————X
Staking	X
Maintenance	X————X

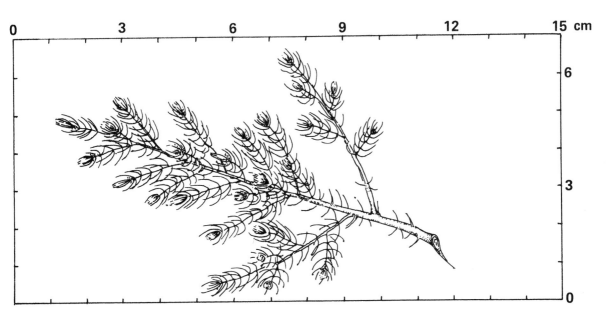

Juniperus recurva – CUPRESSACEAE
Drooping Juniper

A moderately hardy evergreen tree or shrub.
Origin Burma, China and Himalayas.

Uses

The Drooping Juniper can be used as a specimen tree, but the varieties are of even greater value. The Coffin Juniper in particular is effective in the smaller garden. It is taller but narrower than the species, and its bright green drooping shoots are most attractive. *J.r.* 'Embley Park' is excellent in rock gardens.

Description

Dimensions Average ultimate size 4–6m (13–20ft) high by 3–3.5m (10–12ft) wide, but can double these dimensions in good conditions.
Rate of growth Slow.
Life span Variable, but these conifers can be expected to live for 40–50 years or more before starting to decline.
Habit Narrow at first but spreading with age to a broadly pyramidal shape. The branches droop down and have pendulous tips.

Leaves A glaucous grey-green, turning brown with age and retained sometimes for years before falling. This trait is much less evident in the varieties. The foliage clothes the trees from the base upwards.
Flowers Inconspicuous.
Fruits Oval berries brownish at first, turning purplish black in the second year, and up to 10mm (⅜in.) long.
Bark On older trees brown, and tending to peel off in strips, but hidden by foliage.

Features

The branches and shoots have an unusual drooping habit which gives the tree its popular name. This Juniper and its varieties are root- and wind-firm, but are more demanding than many conifers as regards site and climate.
Pollution Fairly tolerant.
Non-poisonous.

Varieties

Juniperus recurva coxii (Coffin Juniper). An attractive narrowly pyramidal tree, more vigorous than the type. Ultimate size 5–6m (17–20ft) high by 1.5–2m (5–7ft) wide. Foliage bright blue-green and

pendulous.
Juniperus recurva 'Embley Park'. A small, spreading shrub 300–450mm (1–1½ft) high by 2–2.5m (7–8ft) wide. The main attraction is the bright, bold green foliage, which is retained year round.

Requirements

Position A sunny but sheltered situation in an area with a moist warm or mild temperate climate suits these conifers best. However, light shade is tolerated in the early years. Hot, dry climates encourage the brown older leaves to remain longer before falling.
Soil A well drained, light to medium loam that is slightly acid to neutral, pH 6.8–7, is most suitable, but this Juniper will tolerate alkaline soil.

Notes on culture

Planting Plant small conifers, up to 900mm (3ft) high, in late summer, early autumn or spring. Staking and tying is not necessary for small plants, but larger ones need support until firmly rooted. Keep the ground around young plants weed-free, well watered and mulched.

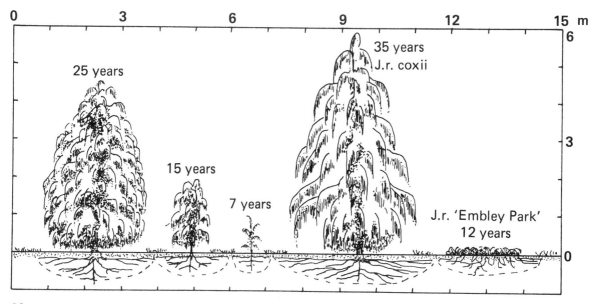

25 years

15 years

7 years

35 years
J.r. coxii

J.r. 'Embley Park'
12 years

Space Allow a minimum area of 4m (13ft) diameter at maturity and a similar distance from buildings. Temporary plantings may be made closer to young Junipers, but filler plants must be removed in good time to prevent overcrowding, which can cause loss of foliage on the lower branches.

Pruning Prune tree forms to limit main shoots to one central leader. Cut back any damaged, diseased or untidy shoots and give an occasional light trim to maintain a good shape. All pruning should be done in spring.

Plant associations J.r. 'Embley Park' provides contrast and interest when planted with other conifers.

Pest and disease control In warm or mild situations Juniper scale, appearing as whitish encrustations on stems and leaves, may cause problems, but it can be controlled by malathion or diazinon sprays. Juniper webber moth caterpillars, which devour the leaves and spin the shoots together with fine webbing, can be controlled by HCH. Rusts, which occur as yellow or orange pustules on leaves, can be checked by spraying with a copper or thiram fungicide.

Season of interest	Winter	Spring	Late spring	Summer	Late summer	Autumn
In full leaf	X———	———	———	———	———	———X
Autumn colour						
Flowers						
Fruits				X———	———X	
Bark and stem						

The following five characteristics determine to a great extent the amount of attention a specific tree requires.

	When planted	5 years	20 years
Height	900 mm	1·5 m	4·0 m
Width	450 mm	1·0 m	2·5 m
Root spread	450 mm	1·5 m	3·5 m
Hardiness	C	C	B/C
Wind-firm	3	2	1/2

Propagation By seed sown in autumn. Named varieties by cuttings taken in late summer or early autumn.

Plant care profile

	Minimum Average High
Site needs	X———X
Soil needs	X
Pruning	X———X
Staking	X———X
Maintenance	X———X

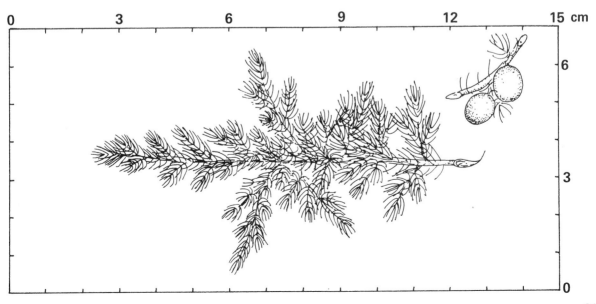

Juniperus sabina – CUPRESSACEAE
Savin, European Savin

A hardy evergreen shrub.
Origin Asia and Europe.

Uses
The Savin and its varieties are particularly valuable in being suitable for formal or informal gardens. They are attractive as specimens, in groups, and in mixed plantings, in small gardens and rock gardens.

Description
Dimensions Under good conditions the Savin can reach an ultimate size of 3–4.5m (10–15ft) high by 2.5–3m (8–10ft) wide, but it is often no more than half that height. This Juniper is usually wider than tall.
Rate of growth Slow to moderate.
Life span Plants can be expected to continue growing for 30 years or more before starting to decline.
Habit Variable, usually broader than tall, with a spreading tendency.
Leaves Of two main types: juvenile, which stand out from the shoots; and adult, which are scale-like and hug the stems of branches. There is also a leaf form intermediate between juvenile and adult leaves.

Flowers Inconspicuous.
Fruits Broadly rounded berries, dark brownish or black and covered with bluish bloom when mature, and about 6mm (¼in.) across.
Bark Relatively insignificant, and usually hidden by foliage.

Features
The Savin and its varieties make outstanding garden subjects. They are comparatively trouble-free, and, given some initial care, need little attention subsequently.
Pollution Tolerant.
Non-poisonous.

Varieties
Juniperus sabina 'Arcadia'. A spreading type of fairly recent introduction. Ultimate size approximately 450–600mm (1½–2ft) high by 2–2.5m (7–8ft) wide. Grey-green foliage, adult in type.
Juniperus sabina 'Blue Danube'. A more vigorous plant, eventually reaching 1.2–1.5m (4–5ft) high by 3–3.5m (10–12ft) wide. Leaves grey-green on top with lighter reverse.

Juniperus sabina 'tamariscifolia' (Spanish Savin). A spreading form, smaller than the preceding varieties. Average ultimate size 600mm (2ft) high by 3m (10ft) wide. Leaves blue or grey-green, and mostly juvenile.

Requirements
Position The Savins are quite accommodating as regards site. A sunny but sheltered position in an area with a warm or mild temperate climate suits these shrubs best, but they can tolerate exposed or lightly shaded situations.
Soil A well drained, light to medium loam that is neutral, pH 7, produces the best specimens, but Savins can grow successfully on quite thin soils over chalk and limestone.

Notes on culture
Planting Plant small conifers, up to 600mm (2ft) high. Late spring is the best time for planting, but good results can also be obtained from plants set out in late summer and early autumn. Staking and tying is not usually necessary. Keep young plants weed-free, well watered and mulched.

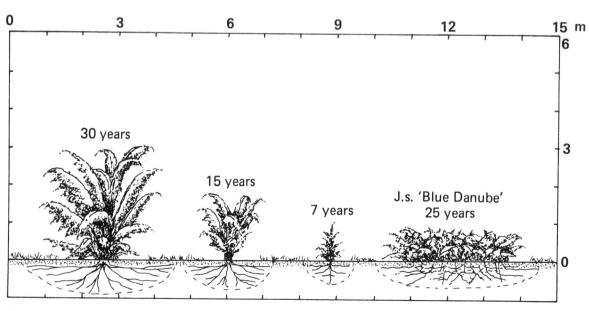

30 years

15 years

7 years

J.s. 'Blue Danube'
25 years

Space Allow each shrub a minimum area equal in diameter to its width at maturity and a similar distance from buildings. Temporary plantings may be made closer to young Junipers, but filler plants must be removed in good time to prevent overcrowding, which can cause loss of foliage on the lower branches.

Pruning Cut back any damaged, diseased or untidy shoots and give an occasional trim as necessary to contain or shape plants. These Junipers will stand a certain amount of cutting. All pruning should be done in late spring.

Plant associations These Junipers look well when planted among shrubs or with rock plants.

Pest and disease control Juniper scale, appearing as whitish encrustations on stems and shoots, can be controlled by malathion or diazinon sprays. Juniper webber moth caterpillars, which devour the leaves and spin the shoots together with fine webbing, can be controlled by HCH. Rusts, which appear as yellow or orange pustules on leaves, can be checked by spraying with a copper or thiram fungicide.

Season of interest	Winter	Spring	Late spring	Summer	Late summer	Autumn
In full leaf	X—					—X
Autumn colour						
Flowers						
Fruits					X——X	
Bark and stem						

The following five characteristics determine to a great extent the amount of attention a specific tree requires.

	When planted	5 years	20 years
Height	600 mm	1·2 m	2·0 m
Width	450 mm	1·0 m	2·0 m
Root spread	450 mm	1·5 m	2·5 m
Hardiness	C	B	B
Wind-firm	2	1	1

Propagation By seed sown in late summer or early autumn. Named varieties by cuttings taken in late summer or early autumn.

Plant care profile

	Minimum	Average	High
Site needs		X	
Soil needs		X	
Pruning	X——X		
Staking	X		
Maintenance	X——X		

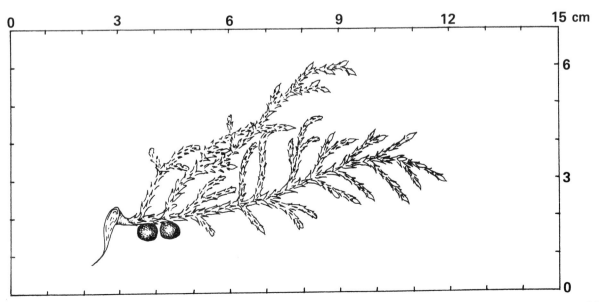

93

Juniperus scopulorum – CUPRESSACEAE
Rocky Mountain Juniper

A hardy evergreen tree.
Origin Western USA.

Uses
The true Rocky Mountain Juniper is little used in present-day gardens, but the varieties are becoming increasingly popular. They are ideal for planting singly as specimens, or together in groups, either alone or with other conifers, in beds, borders, or rock gardens.

Description
Dimensions Variable, but ultimate size rarely exceeds 6m (20ft) high by 2.5m (8ft) wide in gardens.
Rate of growth Slow to moderate.
Life span These conifers can be expected to live for 40 years or more without showing signs of decline.
Habit Variable in the species, but the varieties, which are more often to be seen, are pyramidal in outline.
Leaves Bluish grey, and in older specimens mainly adult. The foliage is fairly open in character.
Flowers Inconspicuous.
Fruits Berries covered with a bluish bloom, ripening in the second year.

Bark Reddish brown, but usually mostly hidden by foliage.

Features
While the type is not widely planted now, the varieties are very attractive and ornamental.
Pollution Tolerant.
Non-poisonous.

Varieties
Juniperus scopulorum 'Blue Heaven'. A narrowly pyramidal tree. Ultimate size 4–5m (13–17ft) high by 900mm–1.2m (3–4ft) wide. Foliage blue-green and fairly open.
Juniperus scopularum 'Springbank'. A narrowly pyramidal form, but slightly wider than *J.s.* 'Blue Heaven'. Ultimate size 4–5m (13–17ft) high by 1.2–1.5m (4–5ft) wide. Foliage a very distinctive blue-grey.

Requirements
Position An open, sunny situation, sheltered from strong winds, in an area with a cool or mild temperate climate suits these plants.
Soil A well drained but moist, light to medium loam that is slightly acid to neutral, pH 6.5–7, is most suitable.

Notes on culture
Planting Plant small trees, up to 900mm (3ft) high. The best planting time is late spring; plants may also be set out in late summer and early autumn, but then protection from strong or freezing winds is desirable. Staking and tying is not necessary for small plants, but larger ones need support until firmly rooted. Keep the ground around young plants weed-free, well watered and mulched.
Space Allow each tree or bush a minimum area equal in diameter to its width at maturity plus 600mm (2ft), and avoid planting closer to buildings than 1.2–1.5m (4–5ft).
Pruning Prune to limit main shoots to one central leader if forking occurs, and cut back any damaged, diseased or untidy shoots to maintain a good shape. This should be done in late spring.
Plant associations This Juniper looks well with other conifers of contrasting shape.

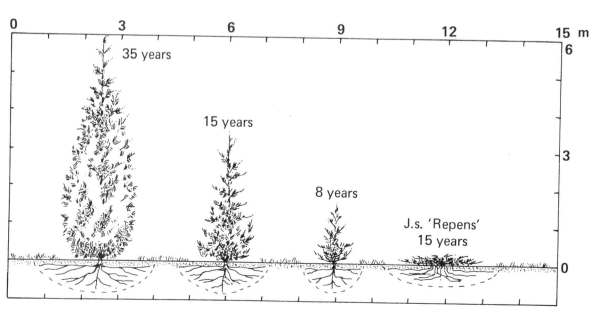

Pest and disease control Juniper scale, appearing as whitish encrustations on stems and leaves, can be controlled by malathion or diazinon sprays. Juniper webber moth caterpillars, which devour the foliage and spin the shoots together with fine webbing, can be controlled by HCH. Rusts, which occur as yellow or orange pustules on leaves, can be checked by spraying with a copper or thiram fungicide.

Propagation By seed sown in early autumn. Named varieties by cuttings taken in late summer or early autumn.

Season of interest	Winter	Spring	Late spring	Summer	Late summer	Autumn
In full leaf	X————					————X
Autumn colour						
Flowers						
Fruits						
Bark and stem						

The following five characteristics determine to a great extent the amount of attention a specific tree requires.

	When planted	5 years	20 years
Height	900 mm	1·5 m	4·0 m
Width	250 mm	450 – 500 mm	1·5 m
Root spread	250 mm	450 – 500 mm	2·0 m
Hardiness	C	B	B
Wind-firm	3	2	1/2

Plant care profile

	Minimum	Average	High
Site needs		X	
Soil needs		X	
Pruning	X		
Staking	X		
Maintenance	X———X		

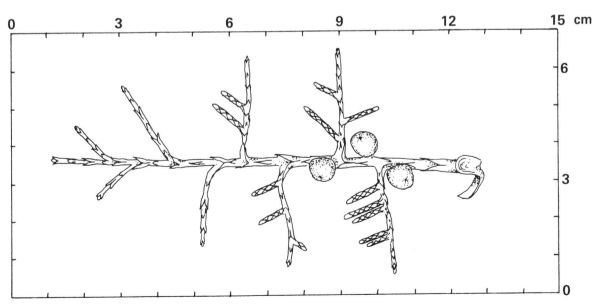

Juniperus squamata – CUPRESSACEAE
Nepal Juniper

A hardy evergreen shrub.
Origin China and Himalayas.

Uses
The varieties of the Nepal Juniper make excellent specimen plants in small gardens, or rock gardens, and they also look very well in mixed plantings.

Description
Dimensions Average ultimate size 750mm (2½ft) high by 1.8–2m (6–7ft) wide, but often rather less.
Rate of growth Slow.
Life span Plants can be expected to continue growing for 30 years or more before starting to decline.
Habit Prostrate.
Leaves Mid-green with a glaucous tinge. The foliage consists of both adult and juvenile leaves.
Flowers Inconspicuous.
Fruits Egg-shaped berries, reddish brown during the first year, turning purplish black as they mature, and about 8mm (⅓ in.) long.
Bark Reddish brown, but usually hidden by foliage.

Features
Some varieties of this Juniper are invaluable for garden purposes, as they provide foliage colourings which are possessed by few other plants.
Pollution Tolerant.
Non-poisonous.

Varieties
Juniperus squamata 'Blue Star'. A fairly recent introduction, with steely grey-blue foliage, growing to about 1.2m (4ft) high.
Juniperus squamata 'Meyeri'. The strongest-growing of this group. Average ultimate size 2.5m (8ft) high by 3m (10ft) wide. Foliage the most intense blue to be found in Junipers.
Juniperus squamata 'Wilsonii'. A rounded or oval shrub, occasionally reaching about 1.8m (6ft) high. Glaucous green foliage which is dense and compact.

Requirements
Position An open, sunny situation, sheltered from cold or strong prevailing winds, in an area with a mild or cool temperate climate suits these plants. Heavy shade should be avoided.

Soil A well drained, light to medium loam that is slightly acid, pH 6.5–6.8, is most suitable. Avoid overfeeding, which causes shoots to develop at the expense of foliage and the colouring to become less intense.

Notes on culture
Planting Plant small conifers, up to 600mm (2ft) high. Late spring is the usual planting time, but good results can also be obtained from plants set out in late summer and early autumn. Staking and tying is not usually necessary. Keep the ground weed-free and mulched within a 600mm (2ft) radius of young plants.
Space Allow an area of 2–3m (7–10ft) in diameter at maturity according to variety and half that distance from buildings. Temporary plantings may be made closer to young Junipers, but filler plants must be removed in good time to prevent overcrowding.

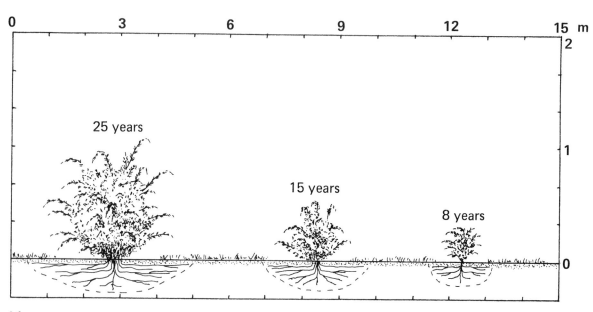

Pruning Cut back any damaged, diseased or untidy shoots to maintain a good shape. Where the foliage is thin or sparse, as in shade, prune to encourage new growth and thickening. In small gardens *J.s.* 'Meyeri' can be contained in a more confined space by cutting back annually or every alternate year. All pruning should be done in late spring.

Plant associations These shrubs look effective when planted among other conifers, or with heathers or rock plants.

Pest and disease control Juniper scale, appearing as whitish encrustations on stems and leaves, can be controlled by malathion or diazinon sprays. Juniper webber moth caterpillars, which devour the leaves and spin the shoots together with fine webbing, can be controlled by HCH. Rusts, which occur as yellow or orange pustules on leaves, can be checked by spraying with a copper or thiram fungicide.

Propagation By seed sown in late summer or early autumn. Named varieties by cuttings taken in late summer or early autumn.

Season of interest	Winter	Spring	Late spring	Summer	Late summer	Autumn
In full leaf	X—					—X
Autumn colour						
Flowers						
Fruits						
Bark and stem	X—					—X

The following five characteristics determine to a great extent the amount of attention a specific tree requires.

	When planted	5 years	20 years
Height	600 mm	650 mm	750 mm
Width	450 mm	1·0 m	2·0 m
Root spread	450 mm	1·2 m	3·0 m
Hardiness	C	B/C	B/C
Wind-firm	3	2	1/2

Plant care profile

	Minimum	Average	High
Site needs		X——X	
Soil needs		X	
Pruning	X		
Staking	X		
Maintenance	X		

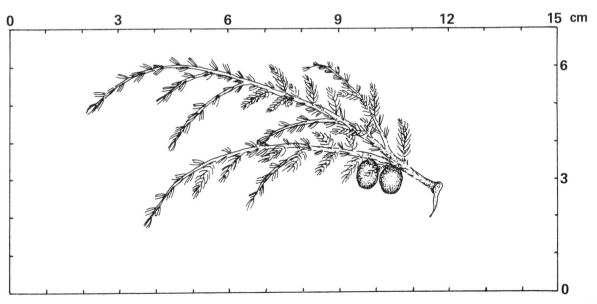

0   3   6   9   12   15 cm

97

Juniperus virginiana – CUPRESSACEAE
Pencil Cedar, Red Cedar

A hardy evergreen tree.
Origin North-eastern USA.

Uses
The Pencil Cedar and its varieties
make handsome specimens. They
are also very effective in groups or
in mixed plantings, and they look
well in rock gardens or near water.

Description
Dimensions Average ultimate size
9m (30ft) high by 5m (17ft) wide.
Rate of growth Slow to moderate.
Life span These conifers can be
expected to live for 50–60 years or
more before declining.
Habit Pyramidal, narrowly in the
early years, broadening with age
and becoming round-topped or
domed.
Leaves Pale to mid-green,
retaining their colour through the
year. The foliage is dimorphic, with
prickly juvenile and smooth adult
leaves occurring simultaneously.
Flowers Rarely occur.
Fruits Rounded berries, usually
covered with a bluish bloom, and
about 6mm (¼ in.) in diameter.
Bark On older conifers dark
brownish grey, and tending to peel
off in strips.

Features
The Pencil Cedar, a Juniper despite
its common name, is one of the
hardiest of conifers, making a root-
and wind-firm tree of considerable
attraction.
Pollution Tolerant.
Non-poisonous.

Varieties
Juniperus virginiana 'Burkii'. A
broadly pyramidal form, reaching
an ultimate size of up to 4m (13ft)
high by 1.8m (6ft) wide. Foliage
blue-grey in summer, turning
purplish in winter.
Juniperus virginiana 'Glauca'. A
form which is columnar in habit,
developing a conical top. Average
ultimate size 5m (17ft) high by
1.5m (5ft) wide. Silver-grey foliage.
Juniperus virginiana 'Globosa'. A
dwarf rounded form which rarely
exceeds 1m (3½ft) high by the
same wide. Grey-green foliage.
Juniperus virginiana 'Skyrocket'.
A narrowly pyramidal tree growing
to 6–7.5m (20–25ft) high by
450–900mm (1½–3ft) wide.
Foliage grey-green in summer,
becoming a stronger green during
late summer and autumn.

Requirements
Position An open, sunny situation,
sheltered from cold winds, suits
these trees. Although all varieties
of the Pencil Cedar are quite hardy,
a lowland area with a warm or mild
temperate climate is best for taller
specimens where a symmetrical
outline is required.
Soil A deep, well drained,
medium loam is most suitable.
These Junipers make good growth
in slightly acid as well as slightly
alkaline conditions, and on soils
over chalk, over a pH range of
6.5–7.5.

Notes on culture
Planting Plant in late summer,
early autumn, or late spring. Small
plants are quicker to become
established: in the case of tree
forms specimens 600–900mm
(2–3ft) high are ideal, and require
no staking and tying. Plants over
1m (3½ft) high need support until
firmly rooted. Keep the ground
around young plants weed-free,
well watered and mulched.
Space Allow the Pencil Cedar a
minimum area of 5m (17ft)
diameter at maturity, and similarly
give the varieties an area equal in
diameter to their ultimate width.
Temporary plantings may be made

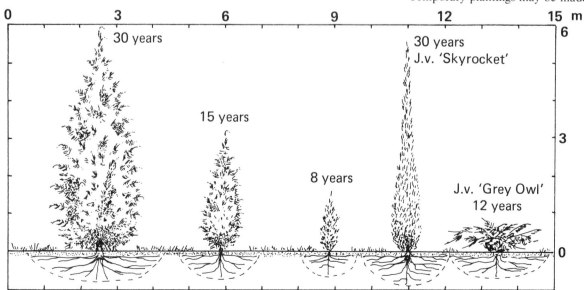

closer to young plants, but filler plants must be removed in good time to prevent overcrowding. Avoid planting tree forms closer to buildings than half the ultimate height of the trees.

Pruning Prune tree forms to limit main shoots to one central leader. On all types cut back any damaged, diseased or untidy shoots. All pruning should be done in late spring.

Plant associations These plants look well among other conifers, or when planted with shrubs, heathers or rock plants.

Pest and disease control Juniper scale, appearing as whitish encrustations on stems and leaves, can be controlled by malathion or diazinon sprays. Juniper webber moth caterpillars, which devour the leaves and spin the shoots together with fine webbing, can be controlled by HCH. Rusts, which occur as yellow or orange pustules on leaves, can be checked by spraying with a copper or thiram fungicide.

Propagation By seed sown in late summer or early autumn – there is always the possibility of an interesting new seedling. Named varieties by cuttings taken in late summer or early autumn.

Season of interest	Winter	Spring	Late spring	Summer	Late summer	Autumn
In full leaf	X————————————————————————X					
Autumn colour						
Flowers						
Fruits				X————X		
Bark and stem						

The following five characteristics determine to a great extent the amount of attention a specific tree requires.

	When planted	5 years	20 years
Height	900 mm	1·8 m	4·0 m
Width	250 mm	450 mm	1·2 m
Root spread	250 mm	500 mm	1·5 m
Hardiness	C	B	B
Wind-firm	2	1	1

Plant care profile

	Minimum Average High
Site needs	X
Soil needs	X
Pruning	X————X
Staking	X
Maintenance	X————X

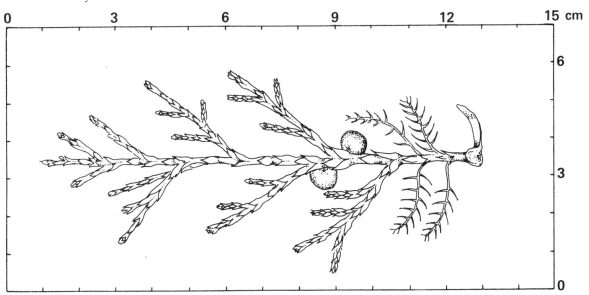

Picea abies – PINACEAE
Norway Spruce

A very hardy evergreen tree.
Origin Western Russia and
Scandinavia.

Uses
The true Norway Spruce can be
grown as a single specimen or be
used for shelter and screening, but
it is too large for most gardens. The
smaller and dwarf varieties are
ideal for garden use as specimens
or in groups. They look well in
rock gardens or near water.

Description
Dimensions Average ultimate size
in gardens 13.5–15m (45–50ft) high
by 4.5–6m (15–20ft) wide.
Rate of growth Moderate to rapid.
Life span Trees reach maturity at
about 40 years old and start to
decline after a further 10–15 years.
Habit Pyramidal, narrowly in the
early years, broadening with age.
Leaves Mid-green to a glossy
deep green, retaining their colour
all the year round.
Flowers Usually inconspicuous.
Fruits Pendulous cones up to
150mm (6in.) long, appearing on
mature trees.
Bark Reddish or orange-brown,
becoming purplish dark grey.

Features
Once beyond the nursery stage the
Norway Spruce is very hardy,
normally moderately root- and
wind-firm in most garden
situations. On very shallow soils
and over chalk in exposed sites tree
forms are less stable.
Pollution Only fairly tolerant.
Non-poisonous.

Varieties
Picea abies 'Acrocona'. Slow
growing, producing distinctive
orange-brown shoot tips.
Picea abies 'Clanbrassilliana'. A
slow-growing form producing a
globose dark green bush. Average
ultimate size 900mm (3ft) high by
the same wide.
Picea abies 'Nidiformis'. A
popular slow-growing form,
broader than tall. Ultimate size
approximately 300–450mm
(1–1½ft) high by 750–900mm
(2½–3ft) wide. Foliage mid-green
with conspicuous brownish buds in
winter.
Picea abies 'Ohlendorfii'.
Slow-growing and of similar height
to *P.a.* 'Clanbrassiliana', but grows
to up to 1.5m (5ft) wide.

Picea abies 'Pumila'. A dwarf,
rounded, compact bush which is
rarely more than 450–600mm
(1½–2ft) high by the same wide.
Branches usually arranged in
horizontal layers.

Requirements
Position The Norway Spruce and
its varieties prefer a cool temperate
climate. They will grow in either
sun or shade, but they need shelter
and protection, especially in the
early years, from strong and
freezing winds.
Soil A deep, well drained but
moist loam that is acid to slightly
acid, pH 6–6.5, is most suitable. On
poor or sandy soils apply a dressing
of 70g per sq. m (2oz. per sq. yd)
of general fertilizer before planting,
and repeat each spring for the first
few years.

Note on culture
Planting Plant between autumn
and spring. Small conifers, about
600–750mm (2–2½ft) high, give
the most satisfactory results, and
even smaller specimens should be
used when transplanting dwarf
varieties. If planted at over 900mm
(3ft) high, taller trees tend to be
unstable at the roots in later years.

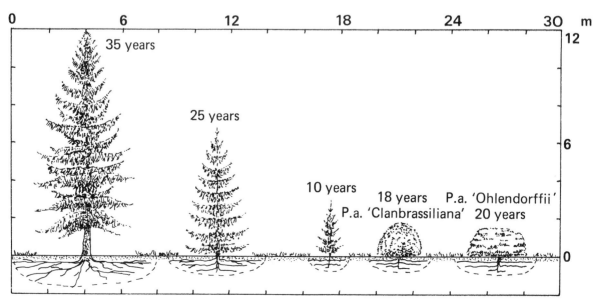

Staking and tying is not necessary for small plants, but larger ones need support.

Space Allow the true Norway Spruce plenty of room if the lowest branches are to be retained: a minimum area of 6m (20ft) diameter is needed at maturity. Avoid planting closer to buildings than 9m (30ft), especially in exposed situations. Dwarf varieties need proportionately less space.

Pruning Prune tree forms to limit main shoots to one central leader. On all types cut back any damaged, diseased or untidy shoots to maintain a good shape. All pruning should be done in late spring.

Plant associations Looks well with heathers.

Pest and disease control Adelges, causing small, pineapple-like swellings on shoots, can be controlled by HCH sprays. Aphids, greenfly and red spider mite can be checked by malathion or dimethoate sprays. Although the Norway Spruce and its varieties can be attacked by various disease organisms, only honey fungus is at all likely to be encountered in garden culture. If planting on land which may have been contaminated, first remove all old tree stumps and sterilize the soil with formaldehyde. Allow four to six weeks for the formaldehyde fumes to dissipate from the soil before planting.

Propagation By seed sown in spring. Named varieties by grafting in spring.

Season of interest	Winter	Spring	Late spring	Summer	Late summer	Autumn
In full leaf	X———————————————————————X					
Autumn colour						
Flowers						
Fruits				X—————————X		
Bark and stem	X———————————————————————X					

The following five characteristics determine to a great extent the amount of attention a specific tree requires.

	When planted	5 years	20 years
Height	600 mm	1·5 m	6·0 m
Width	200 mm	500 mm	2·0 m
Root spread	200 mm	750 mm	3·0 m
Hardiness	B	A/B	A
Wind-firm	3	3	2

Plant care profile

	Minimum	Average	High
Site needs		X	
Soil needs		X———X	
Pruning	X———X		
Staking	X		
Maintenance	X———X		

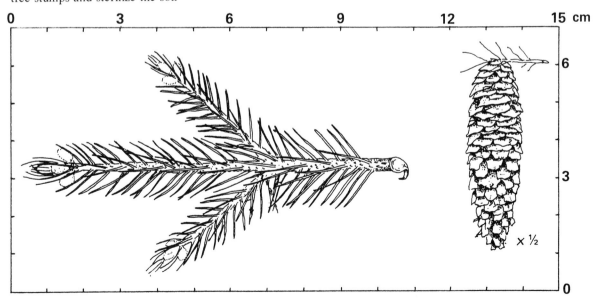

× ½

Picea breweriana – PINACEAE
Brewer's Weeping Spruce

A moderately hardy tree.
Origin   Western north USA.

Uses
Brewer's Weeping Spruce is outstanding as a specimen tree when planted in grass, or as the focal point of a plot. It is most suitable for medium or large gardens, where it can be seen to good effect.

Description
Dimensions   Average ultimate size in gardens 9m (30ft) high by 4–5m (13–17ft) wide. Trees in the wild often grow much larger.
Rate of growth   Slow to moderate.
Life span   Trees reach maturity at about 35 years old and continue growing for many years beyond.
Habit   Broadly pyramidal and typically weeping in character, with branches carrying pendulous shoots which are very long and slender, sometimes 2–3m (7–10ft) long and little thicker than a pencil.
Leaves   Dark green with silvery grey or grey-green reverse, giving an over-all grey-green effect.
Flowers   Inconspicuous.
Fruits   Cones which are green, turning purplish brown, and 75mm (3in.) or more in length, appearing after the trees are 25 years old.

Bark   Not particularly outstanding, usually screened by curtains of green foliage.

Features
Brewer's Weeping Spruce makes a most handsome tree, and given suitable site and soil conditions is root- and wind-firm.
Pollution   Fairly tolerant.
Non-poisonous.

Varieties
There do not appear to be any outstanding varieties or selections of this species.

Requirements
Position   A sheltered situation, protected from strong and freezing winds, in an area with a moist mild temperate climate suits this tree. A sunny situation is best, but light shade is acceptable. Young trees in particular tolerate light shade well.
Soil   A deep, well drained but moist loam that is slightly acid, pH around 6.5, is ideal. Sandy soils can be made suitable by the addition of well rotted manure or organic matter.

Notes on culture
Planting   Plant small trees, 600–900mm (2–3ft) high. Late spring is the best time for planting, but given suitable conditions and some protection young trees can be successfully moved during autumn and winter. Staking and tying is usually beneficial for small plants, and is essential for trees over 1m (3½ft) high until they are well established. Support the main stem until it is the required height, to overcome the weeping tendency of the central leader.
Space   Allow a minimum area of 5m (17ft) diameter, and preferably more, to display each tree to advantage. Avoid planting closer to buildings or boundary fences than about 4m (13ft).
Pruning   Prune to limit main shoots to one central leader, and trim occasionally to maintain a good shape. All pruning should be done in late spring.
Plant associations   Most effective as a specimen in turf.

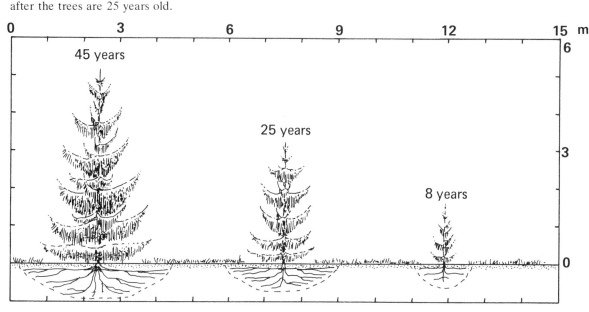

45 years

25 years

8 years

Pest and disease control Adelges, causing small, pineapple-like swellings on shoots, can be controlled by HCH sprays. Aphids, greenfly and red spider mite can be checked by malathion or dimethoate sprays. Honey fungus occasionally attacks young trees. If planting on land which may have been contaminated, first remove all old tree stumps and sterilize the soil with formaldehyde. Allow four to six weeks for the formaldehyde fumes to dissipate from the soil before planting.
Propagation By seed sown in spring. Trees with particularly desirable characteristics by grafting in spring.

Season of interest	Winter	Spring	Late spring	Summer	Late summer	Autumn
In full leaf	X———————————————————————————————X					
Autumn colour						
Flowers						
Fruits				X—————————X		
Bark and stem						

The following five characteristics determine to a great extent the amount of attention a specific tree requires.

	When planted	5 years	20 years
Height	900 mm	1·5 m	3·0 m
Width	400 mm	600 mm	1·2 m
Root spread	400 mm	750 mm	1·5 m
Hardiness	C	C	B/C
Wind-firm	3	2/3	2

Plant care profile

	Minimum	Average	High
Site needs		X———X	
Soil needs		X———X	
Pruning	X———X		
Staking	X———X		
Maintenance	X———X		

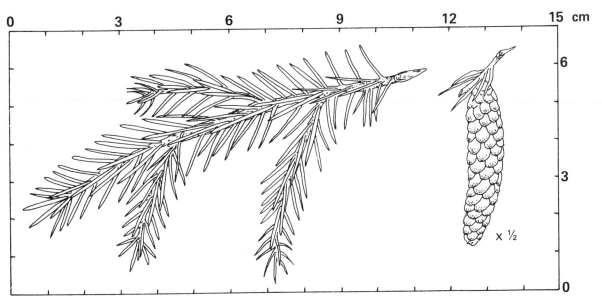

x ½

Picea glauca – PINACEAE
Alberta Spruce, White Spruce

A very hardy evergreen tree.
Origin Canada and northern USA.

Uses
The true Canadian Spruce is only suitable for medium to large gardens. The dwarf varieties can be used individually as specimens, collectively in groups, in beds, or in mixed plantings. They are also excellent for planting in rock gardens, or even in containers.

Description
Dimensions Variable, although the average ultimate size in gardens is 7.5m (25ft) high by 2.5–2.7m (8–9ft) wide, this spruce can more than double the size given in good conditions.
Rate of growth Slow.
Life span These conifers live for upwards of 80 years.
Habit Pyramidal, narrowly in the early years, broadening slightly with age.
Leaves Grey-green.
Flowers Inconspicuous.
Fruits Brown cones, up to 60mm (2½in.) long, appearing on mature trees.
Bark Grey-brown and scaly.

Features
The type needs more space than is usually available in gardens, unlike the varieties which are excellent.
Pollution Only fairly tolerant.
Non-poisonous.

Varieties
Picea glauca albertiana 'Conica'. An excellent dwarf form, rarely exceeding about 1.5m (5ft) high by 750mm (2½ft) wide and forming a dense, compact pyramid. Foliage a soft light green.
Picea glauca 'Nana'. Slightly smaller than *P.g. albertiana* 'Conica', this dwarf conifer attains an average ultimate size of 900mm (3ft) high by 750mm (2½ft) wide. Rounded habit and grey-blue foliage.

Requirements
Position A sunny or lightly shaded situation in an area with a mild or cool and preferably moist temperate climate suits these Spruces. Protection from severe frost and cold winds is necessary, especially for young plants.

Soil A deep, well drained but moist, light to medium loam, moderately to slightly acid, pH 6–6.5, is most suitable. These Spruces require phosphates and nitrogen to ensure steady growth. Before planting apply a dressing of 70g per sq. m (2oz. per sq. yd) of general fertilizer, and on poor soils repeat annually in spring. On land of average fertility dressings can be given in alternate years.

Notes on culture
Planting Plant small conifers up to 900mm (3ft) high or half to one-third that height for dwarf varieties, in autumn, winter or (preferably) spring. Staking and tying is not necessary for small plants, but trees over 900mm (3ft) high need support until firmly rooted.
Space Allow the true Alberta Spruce a minimum area of 3m (10ft) diameter at maturity, and avoid planting closer to buildings than 5m (17ft). Dwarf varieties need an area equal to their width. Avoid overcrowding.

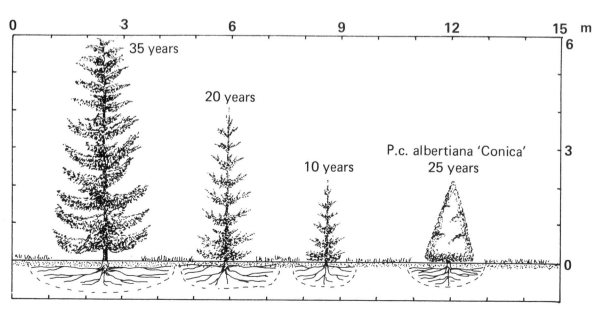

Pruning Prune tree forms to limit main shoots to one central leader. The dwarf varieties can be allowed to grow without restricting the number of stems. On all types cut back any damaged, diseased or untidy shoots to maintain a good shape. All pruning should be done in spring.

Plant associations The type is seen to best effect in turf. The dwarf varieties look well with heathers or rock plants.

Pest and desease control Adelges. causing small, pineapple-like swellings on shoots, can be controlled by HCH sprays. Conifer spinning mite, occurring as reddish orange grubs, usually among strands of fine webbing, can be checked by malathion sprays. Red spider mite and other mites often attack *P.g. albertiana* 'Conica' but can be checked by malathion or dimethoate sprays. Spruce aphid may considerably weaken dwarf varieties, but can be controlled by malathion or dimethoate.

Propagation By seed sown in spring. Named varieties by cuttings taken in late summer.

Season of interest	Winter	Spring	Late spring	Summer	Late summer	Autumn
In full leaf	X———————————————————————————————X					
Autumn colour						
Flowers						
Fruits				X———————X		
Bark and stem						

The following five characteristics determine to a great extent the amount of attention a specific tree requires.

	When planted	5 years	20 years
Height	900 mm	1·5 m	4·0 m
Width	300 mm	500 mm	1·5 m
Root spread	300 mm	750 mm	2·0 m
Hardiness	B	B	A/B
Wind-firm	2	1/2	1

Plant care profile

	Minimum	Average	High
Site needs		X	
Soil needs		X———X	
Pruning	X———X		
Staking	X———X		
Maintenance	X———————————————X		

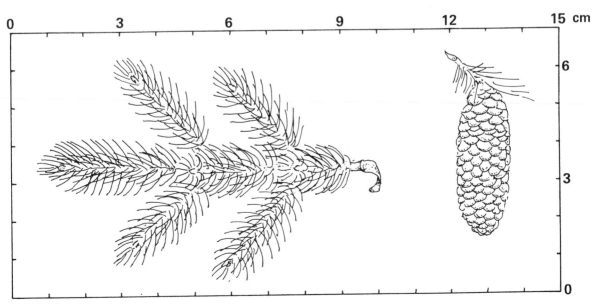

Picea omorika – PINACEAE
Serbian Spruce

A very hardy evergreen tree.
Origin Europe.

Uses
The Serbian Spruce and its varieties make impressive specimens when planted singly in grass. The dwarf variety looks well in rock gardens. The fact that it is one of the few conifers which can tolerate pullution makes the Serbian Spruce particularly useful in town and suburban situations.

Description
Dimensions Average ultimate size 13.5–15m (45–50ft) high by 2.5–3m (8–10ft) wide.
Rate of growth Moderate to rapid.
Life span Trees can have a useful garden life of 30–40 years or more.
Habit Narrowly pyramidal with short branches, the lowest of which are gracefully curving and upswept.
Leaves Glossy dark green, with white to pale green reverse.
Flowers The female flowers are bright reddish shades, and usually produced near the top of the tree. The male flowers are usually inconspicuous.
Fruits Purple cones, 50mm (2in.) long.

Bark Orange-brown, flaking off into square pieces.

Features
The Serbian Spruce is one of the very few forest trees which can be comfortably grown in all but the smallest gardens.
Pollution Tolerates a certain degree of smoke and pollution.
Non-poisonous.

Varieties
Picea omorika 'Nana'. A dwarf form which makes a rounded bush with close-knit, compact foliage.
Picea omorika 'Pendula'. A slender form with drooping, pendulous branches. Ultimate size approximately 12m (40ft) high by 2.5m (8ft) wide.

Requirements
Position The Serbian Spruce and its varieties grow well in sun or light shade, but a situation sheltered from strong and cold winds is preferable. Young trees are vulnerable to late spring frosts. A moist mild temperate climate encourages quick growth and development.

Soil The best trees are to be found on deep, well drained but moist, medium loams that are slightly acid, pH 6.5, but the Serbian Spruce can grow satisfactorily on drier and more alkaline chalk and limestone soils.

Notes on culture
Planting Plant small trees, preferably not more than 600–900mm (2–3ft) high, in autumn, winter or spring. The bush variety can safely be planted when smaller still, at 300–450mm (12–18in.) high or less. Staking and tying is not neccessary for small plants, but larger trees need support until firmly rooted. Keep the ground weed-free, well watered and mulched within a 600mm (2ft) radius of young plants.
Space Allow a minimum area of 4m (13ft) diameter at maturity, and avoid planting closer to buildings than about 6m (20ft).
Pruning Prune to limit main shoots to one central leader. This should be done in late spring.
Plant associations The type species is effective in grass as a specimen. The dwarf variety associates well with other conifers and with rock plants.

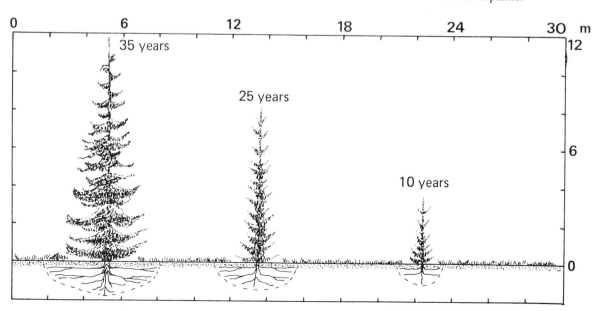

Pest and disease control Although the Serbian Spruce can be attacked by most of the ailments which afflict Spruces in general, on the whole it is rarely affected by anything except honey fungus. Unfortunately this Spruce does seem to be particulary prone to infection by honey fungus. If planting on land which may have been contaminated, first remove all old tree stumps and sterilize the soil with formaldehyde. Allow four to six weeks for the formaldehyde fumes to dissipate from the soil before planting.
Propagation By seed sown in spring. Named varieties by cuttings taken in late summer or grafting in spring.

Season of interest	Winter	Spring	Late spring	Summer	Late summer	Autumn
In full leaf	X					X
Autumn colour						
Flowers						
Fruits				X		X
Bark and stem	X					X

The following five characteristics determine to a great extent the amount of attention a specific tree requires.

	When planted	5 years	20 years
Height	600 mm	2·0 m	7·5 m
Width	100 mm	300 mm	1·2 m
Root spread	150 mm	450 mm	1·5 m
Hardiness	B	A/B	A
Wind-firm	2	1/2	1

Plant care profile

	Minimum	Average	High
Site needs		X	
Soil needs		X	
Pruning	X		
Staking	X		
Maintenance	X——X		

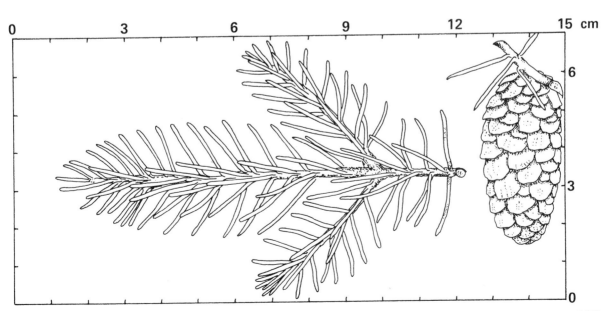

Picea orientalis – PINACEAE
Oriental Spruce

A moderately hardy evergreen tree.
Origin Caucasus and Asia.

Uses
The Oriental Spruce makes a fine specimen for medium to large gardens, and the variety *P.o.* 'Aurea' is excellent for all but the smallest plots.

Description
Dimensions Average ultimate size 15m (50ft) high by 6m (20ft) wide.
Rate of growth Slow at first, moderate after the first few years.
Life span Variable. On dry, shallow ground trees can be past their best at 25 years old, but live to twice this age on fertile moist land and retain their good qualites.
Habit Pyramidal, with a spiky top but thick foliage near the base.
Leaves Glossy dark green short needles.
Flowers Inconspicuous.
Fruits Cones which are an attractive purple, turning grey-brown, and up to 50–75mm (2–3in.) long, appearing when the trees are about 20 years old and upwards.
Bark Grey, speckled and rough when young, turning pink and brown as it ages.

Features
Conspicuous, spiky foliage at the top, making this quite distinctive.
Pollution Fairly tolerant.
Non-poisonous.

Varieties
Picea orientalis 'Aurea'. A form which is pyramidal in habit and slower-growing than the species, eventually reaching about 7.5–9m (25–30ft) high by up to 3.5m (12ft) wide. Foliage yellow in spring, turning greenish in summer.
Picea orientalis 'Pendula'. A pendulous, pyramidal form which has dark green foliage.

Requirements
Position A sunny or lightly shaded situation, well protected from freezing winds, in an area with a moist mild temperate climate suits these trees. On sites which suffer from late spring frosts young trees need shelter for the first few years.
Soil A well drained, light to medium loam which provides a deep, moist rootrun and is slightly acid, pH 6–6.5, is most suitable. On sandy soils apply a dressing of 70g per sq. m (2oz. per sq. yd) of general fertilizer before planting, and repeat each spring.

Notes on culture
Planting Plant small trees, up to 900mm (3ft) high, during autumn, winter or spring. Spring is usually best, provided that watering can be carried out in dry weather. Staking and tying is not necessary for small plants, but larger trees need support until firmly rooted.
Space Allow the Oriental Spruce a minimum area of 6m (20ft) diameter at maturity, and avoid planting closer to buildings than about 7.5m (25ft). *P.o.* 'Aurea' needs only about 4m (13ft) diameter.
Pruning Prune to limit main shoots to one central leader, and cut back any damaged, diseased or untidy shoots to maintain a good shape. All pruning should be done in late spring.
Plant associations This Spruce mixes well with small conifers or can be shown to good effect in turf.

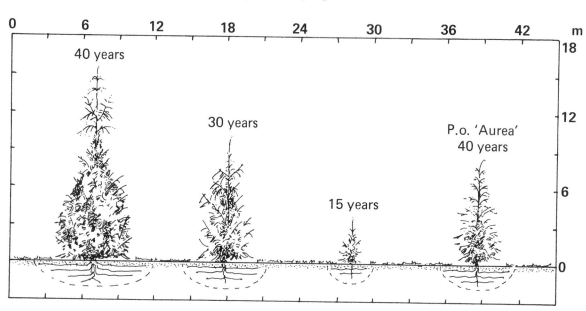

Pest and disease control Given good cultivation and so long as the tree does not have to endure extremes of heat or cold, wet or dry, few problems should arise. Adelges, which sometimes occur as small, pineapple-like swellings on shoots, can be controlled by HCH sprays. Aphids, which increase rapidly during warm weather, and red spider mite, which is usually worst in hot, dry weather, can both be checked by malathion or dimethoate sprays. Honey fungus occasionally kills young trees. If planting on land which may have been contaminated, first remove all old tree stumps and sterilize the soil with formaldehyde. Allow four to six weeks for the formaldehyde fumes to dissipate from the soil before planting.
Propagation By seed sown in spring. Named varieties by grafting in spring.

Season of interest	Winter	Spring	Late spring	Summer	Late summer	Autumn
In full leaf	X————————————————————————————X					
Autumn colour						
Flowers						
Fruits				X————————————X		
Bark and stem	X————————————————————————————X					

The following five characteristics determine to a great extent the amount of attention a specific tree requires.

	When planted	5 years	20 years
Height	600 mm	1·5 m	6·0 m
Width	250 mm	500 mm	2·5 m
Root spread	250 mm	750 mm	3·0 m
Hardiness	C	C	B/C
Wind-firm	3	2	1/2

Plant care profile

	Minimum Average High
Site needs	X————X
Soil needs	X————X
Pruning	X————X
Staking	X
Maintenance	X————X

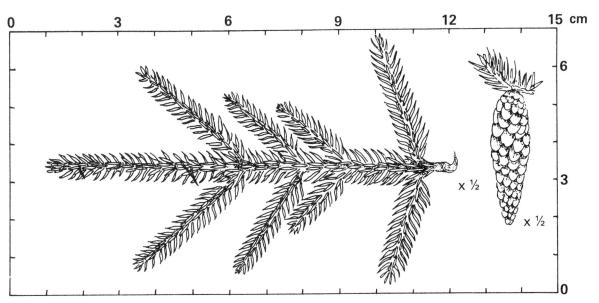

x ½

x ½

Picaea pungens – PINACEAE
Colorado Spruce

A moderately hardy evergreen tree.
Origin USA.

Uses
Most of the varieties of the Colorado Spruce make attractive and imposing specimens, but they need a large or medium garden. The dwarf form, however, is ideal for beds or for rock gardens.

Description
Dimensions Variable, but ultimate size of 9m (30ft) high by 3.5m (12ft) wide in gardens, can be greatly exceeded.
Rate of growth Slow to moderate.
Life span Trees reach maturity at 20–25 years old, but continue to grow for a further 20 or so years before starting to decline.
Habit Variable, but usually narrowly pyramidal when young, spreading with age.
Leaves Needles which radiate from thick shoots, and are light grey-blue to almost white at first, later turning to dark blue-green. The winter buds are fairly prominent and brownish yellow. The foliage tends to be thicker in grafted plants than in those raised from seed.
Flowers Inconspicuous.

Fruits Cones which are blue-green initially, later turning light brown with leathery scales, appear when the trees are about 20 years old.
Bark Mostly hidden by branches and foliage.

Features
The species and varieties make large trees, needing considerable space, but are excellent where there is room to grow.
Pollution Fairly tolerant.
Non-poisonous.

Varieties
Picea pungens 'Endtz'. A neat, narrowly pyramidal tree which occasionally reaches 7.5–9m (25–30ft) high by 4–5m (13–17ft.) wide. Very blue foliage.
Picea pungens glauca (Blue Spruce). Glaucous grey-blue foliage.
Picea pungens 'Globosa'. A rather slow-growing dwarf bush type. This rarely exceeds 1m (3½ft) high by 600mm–900mm (2–3ft) wide.
Picea pungens 'Koster'. (Koster Blue Spruce). A very popular form, pyramidal in habit. Average ultimate size 7–9m (23–30ft) high by 4–4.5m (13–15ft) wide. Silvery blue foliage.

Picea pungens 'Moerheimii'. An outstanding form, a blue-green pyramid of foliage with the branches usually arranged in tiers. Approximate ultimate size 9–10.5m (30–35ft) high by 5–6m (17–20ft) wide.

Requirements
Position A sunny but sheltered situation in an area with a cool or mild temperate climate suits these trees. These Spruces can tolerate slightly drier and colder conditions than some others, but young trees need protection from frost and freezing winds.
Soil A deep, well drained, medium loam that is acid to slightly acid, pH 6–6.5, is most suitable.

Notes on culture
Planting Plant small trees, 600–900mm (2–3ft) high, in autumn, winter or spring. Staking and tying is not necessary for small plants, but larger trees need support until firmly rooted. Keep the ground around young plants well watered and mulched.

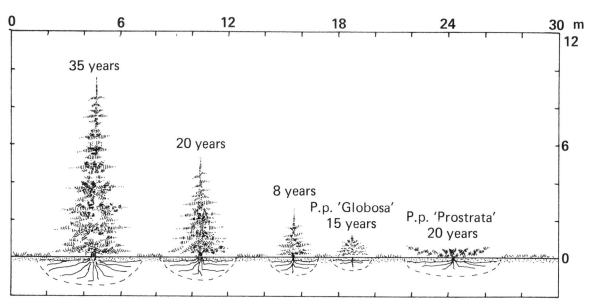

35 years

20 years

8 years
P.p. 'Globosa'
15 years

P.p. 'Prostrata'
20 years

Space Allow each tree a minimum area of a diameter equal to its width at maturity, and avoid planting tall forms closer to buildings than 7.5m (25ft).
Pruning Prune to limit main shoots to one central leader, and cut back any damaged. diseased or untidy shoots to maintain a good shape. All pruning should be done in late spring.
Plant associations Large trees are most effective in grass. The dwarf variety is excellent among mixed evergreens, or with rock plants.
Pest and disease control Adelges, causing small, pineapple-like swellings on shoots, can be controlled by HCH sprays. Aphids, greenfly and red spider mite can be checked by malathion or dimethoate sprays. Honey fungus can attack these Spruces. If planting on land which may have been contaminated, first remove all old tree stumps and sterilize the soil with formaldehyde. Allow four to six weeks for the formaldehyde fumes to dissipate from the soil.
Propagation By seed sown in spring. Named varieties by cuttings taken in late summer or by grafting in spring.

Season of interest	Winter	Spring	Late spring	Summer	Late summer	Autumn
In full leaf	X———					——X
Autumn colour						
Flowers						
Fruits				X———		——X
Bark and stem	———X				X———	

The following five characteristics determine to a great extent the amount of attention a specific tree requires.

	When planted	5 years	20 years
Height	600mm	1·8 m	6·0 m
Width	200mm	750mm	2·5 m
Root spread	200mm	900mm	3·0 m
Hardiness	C	B	A/B
Wind-firm	2/3	2	1/2

Plant care profile

	Minimum Average High
Site needs	X———X
Soil needs	X
Pruning	X———X
Staking	X———X
Maintenance	X———X

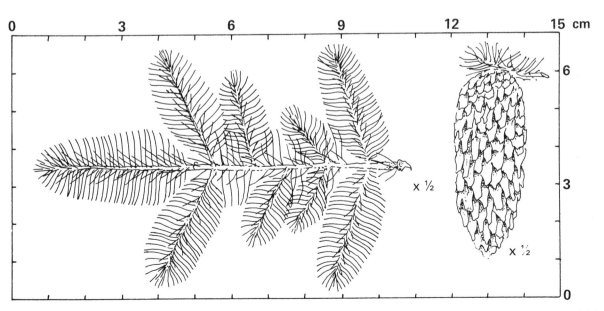

x ½

x ½

0   3   6   9   12   15 cm

Pinus aristata – PINACEAE
Bristlecone Pine

A moderately hardy evergreen tree or shrub.
Origin   USA.

Uses
The Bristlecone Pine looks well in mixed plantings, in beds or in rock gardens.

Description
Dimensions   Some very old specimens are no more than 3–4m (10–13ft) high by 1.5–2m (5–7ft) wide.
Rate of growth   Slow to very slow.
Life span   This Pine is one of the longest-lived plants known to man. Some specimens are believed to be as much as 4,000 years old, or even more.
Habit   Pyramidal when grown as a single-stemmed tree. Shrub forms are more irregular in shape.
Leaves   Arranged rosette-fashion in groups of five, and usually spotted with whitish resin.
Flowers   Inconspicuous.
Fruits   Cones which are brownish when ripe, 50–75mm (2–3in.) long, and have long, thin prickles attached.
Bark   Reddish brown, but often concealed by foliage.

Features
The leaves at the ends of the shoots are arranged in rosettes like brush bristles, hence its name.
Pollution   Moderately tolerant.
Non-poisonous.

Varieties
Despite the antiquity of the Bristlecone Pine, there do not appear to be any readily available varieties.

Requirements
Position   A fairly open, sunny but sheltered situation well protected from cold or strong prevailing winds is most suitable for this conifer and a warm or mild temperate climate is essential for good growth.
Soil   A well drained, light to medium loam that is acid, pH 6–6.5, is most suitable.

Notes on culture
Planting   Plant small conifers, up to 450mm (1½ft) high, in autumn, winter or spring. Staking and tying is not necessary for small plants, but larger specimens need support until firmly rooted. Keep the ground weed-free, well watered and mulched within a 600mm (2ft) radius of 'young' plants.
Space   In view of the slow growth rate and provided other plants are not allowed to encroach, little additional space is likely to be required until the far distant future. Allow each tree a 3m (10ft) diameter and similar distance from buildings.
Pruning   If a single-stem form is wanted prune to limit main shoots to one central leader. On all types cut back any damaged or diseased shoots. All pruning should be done in late spring.
Plant associations   The Bristlecone Pine looks effective when planted among mixed conifers, or with heathers or rock plants.

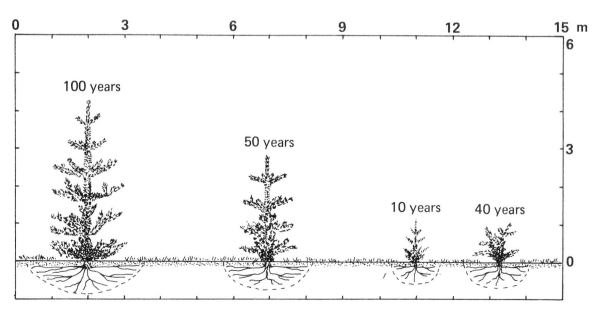

Pest and disease control Adelges, which feed on stems and foliage, producing waxy, whitish, wool-like tufts, are best treated individually if possible on small specimens. Paint the affected area with HCH, and to prevent future outbreaks, spray the whole tree or shrub each spring with HCH. Pine shoot moth caterpillars can burrow into the terminal shoots, killing growth above the point of entry. HCH sprays applied each spring should prevent an attack. There is no real cure once the insects have burrowed inside the shoots. Sawfly larvae can feed on the foliage and should be promptly dealt with, using sprays of fenitrothion or malathion. Canker and dieback sometimes attack trees, usually following injury or malnutrition. Cut out the affected area and spray with benomyl fungicide. Honey fungus can kill young trees. If planting on land which may have been contaminated, first remove all old tree stumps and sterilize the soil with formaldehyde. Allow four to six weeks for the formaldehyde fumes to dissipate from the soil before planting.
Propagation By seed sown in spring.

Season of interest	Winter	Spring	Late spring	Summer	Late summer	Autumn
In full leaf	X———					——X
Autumn colour						
Flowers						
Fruits					X——	——X
Bark and stem						

The following five characteristics determine to a great extent the amount of attention a specific tree requires.

	When planted	5 years	20 years
Height	600 mm	900 mm	1·5 m
Width	200 mm	350 mm	600 mm
Root spread	200 mm	450 mm	750 mm
Hardiness	C	C	B/C
Wind-firm	3	3	2

Plant care profile

	Minimum	Average	High
Site needs		X——	——X
Soil needs		X	
Pruning	X——	——X	
Staking	X		
Maintenance	X		

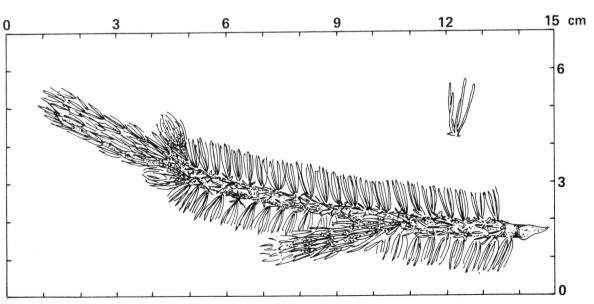

Pinus cembra – PINACEAE

Arolla Pine

A hardy evergreen tree or shrub.
Origin Europe.

Uses
The Arolla Pine and its varieties
make pleasing specimens for large
and medium gardens.

Description
Dimensions Average ultimate size
in gardens 6–7.5m (20–25ft) high
by 2.5–3m (8–10ft) wide.
Rate of growth Slow.
Life span Variable. Some conifers
live for upwards of 100 years,
others die quite suddenly when less
than 40 years old.
Habit Usually pyramidal, but can
be columnar with a rounded top.
Leaves Needle-like, dark green on
the upper surface with bluish pale
green or white reverse, and
arranged in pairs.
Flowers Inconspicuous.
Fruits Cones which are purplish
when ripe and normally about
50mm (2in.) long, carried on older
trees.
Bark Greyish brown.

Features
The Arolla Pine is an attractive
conifer, and able to withstand a
fairly wide range of conditions.
Pollution Fairly tolerant.
Non-poisonous.

Varieties
Pinus cembra 'Aureovariegata'.
Less vigorous than the species. The
foliage is, as the name implies,
marked green and gold.
Pinus cembra 'Stricta'. A narrow
columnar form.

Requirements
Position A sunny, open situation
in an area with a mild or cool
temperate climate suits these trees.
The Arolla Pine will tolerate a fair
amount of exposure to wind
without much harm.
Soil A well drained, acid loam,
pH 6 or near, as a rule gives good
results. On poor or sandy soils
apply a dressing of 70g per sq. m
(2oz. per sq. yd) of general
fertilizer before planting, and
repeat each spring.

Notes on culture
Planting Plant small conifers, up
to 600mm (2ft) high. Autumn is
the best time for planting, but
plants can also be successfully
moved during fine weather in
winter and spring. Staking and
tying is not necessary. Keep the
ground around young plants
weed-free and well watered.
Space Allow a minimum area of
3m (10ft) diameter at maturity, and
avoid planting tall forms closer to
buildings than 6m (20ft).
Pruning Prune tree forms to limit
main shoots to one central leader.
On all types cut back any damaged,
diseased or untidy shoots to
maintain a good shape. All pruning
should be done in late spring.
Plant associations These Pines
associate well with other conifers,
shrubs and heathers.

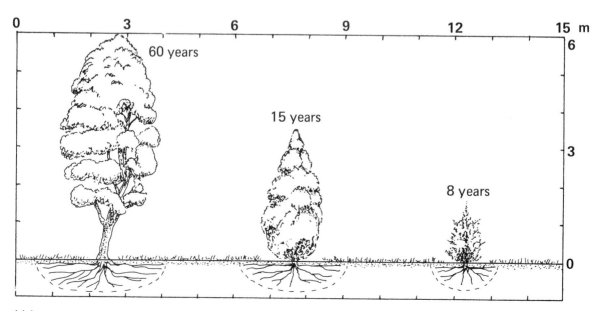

Pest and disease control Although the Arolla Pine and its varieties are not greatly troubled by pests or diseases, they can be affected by some of the problems which tend to beset Pines. Control adelges by spraying with HCH, repeating the following year in spring as a preventive measure. Spring sprays of HCH should also prevent attacks of Pine shoot moth caterpillars. Sawfly larvae can be controlled by sprays of fenitrothion or malathion. To check canker and dieback cut out affected parts and spray with benomyl. If planting on land which may have been contaminated with honey fungus, first remove all old tree stumps and sterilize the soil with formaldehyde. Allow four to six weeks for the formaldehyde fumes to dissipate from the soil before planting.

Propagation By seed sown in spring. Named varieties, which do not breed true from seed, by grafting in spring

Season of interest	Winter	Spring	Late spring	Summer	Late summer	Autumn
In full leaf	X——	———	———	———	———	——X
Autumn colour						
Flowers						
Fruits				X——	———	——X
Bark and stem						

The following five characteristics determine to a great extent the amount of attention a specific tree requires.

	When planted	5 years	20 years
Height	600 mm	1·8 m	4·5 m
Width	250 mm	1·0 m	2·0 m
Root spread	250 mm	1·5 m	2·5 m
Hardiness	C	B	B
Wind-firm	3	2	1

Plant care profile

	Minimum	Average	High
Site needs		X——	——X
Soil needs		X	
Pruning	X——	——X	
Staking	X		
Maintenance	X——	——X	

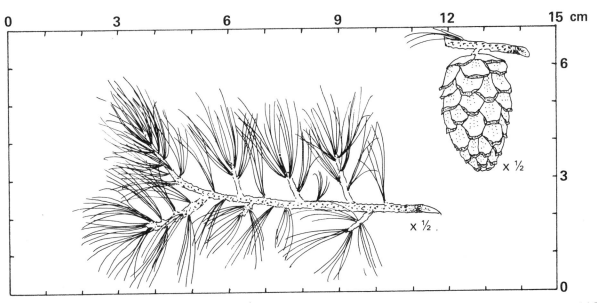

x ½

x ½

0   3   6   9   12   15 cm

6

3

0

Pinus heldreichi leucodermis – PINACEAE
Bosnian Pine

A hardy evergreen tree.
Origin Europe.

Uses
The Bosnian Pine makes a fine specimen for large and medium gardens. The dwarf forms are effective in rock gardens.

Description
Dimensions Average ultimate size in gardens 9m (30ft) high by 4.5m (15ft) wide. Trees in the wild often grow much larger.
Rate of growth Slow to moderate.
Life span Variable, but these Pines can be expected to live for 50 years or more before starting to decline.
Habit Sometimes variable, but typically narrowly pyramidal in the early years, broadening later.
Leaves Long-lasting dark green needles, about 100–125mm (4–5in.) long and arranged in pairs.
Flowers Inconspicuous.
Fruits Oval cones which are blue-purple when young, turning brown on ripening, and up to 75mm (3in.) long.
Bark Dull grey and fairly smooth, with criss-crossing fine cracks.

Features
Lighter foliage effect than many pines provide and more elegant. Very hardy, usually wind- and root-firm, and need little attention.
Pollution Fairly tolerant.
Non-poisonous.

Varieties
Pinus leucodermis 'Compact Gem'. A rounded ball of dark green foliage, roughly as wide as tall. Approximate ultimate size 1.5m (5ft) high by the same wide.
Pinus leucodermis 'Pygmy'. Similar to *P.l.* 'Compact Gem', but foliage thicker and of a lighter green.

Requirements
Position A mild or cool temperate climate suits this mountain Pine best, although it is quite hardy. An open situation, receiving full sun for most of the day, will encourage compact, even growth.

Soil A well drained, slightly acid loam, pH 6.5, is ideal. However, this Pine can tolerate chalky soil better than many other members of the genus. On poor soils the true Bosnian Pine will benefit from an annual spring dressing of 70g per sq. m (2oz. per sq. yd) of general fertilizer for the first few years.

Notes on culture
Planting Plant small conifers, up to 450–600mm (1½–2ft) high. Autumn is the best time for planting, but plants can also be moved in winter and spring. Staking and tying is not usually necessary. Keep the ground around young plants weed-free and mulched.
Space Allow each tree or shrub a minimum area equal in diameter to its width at maturity. Avoid planting the species closer to buildings than 6m (20ft).
Pruning Prune tree forms to limit main shoots to one central leader. On all types cut back any damaged, diseased or untidy shoots to maintain a good shape. All pruning should be done in late spring.

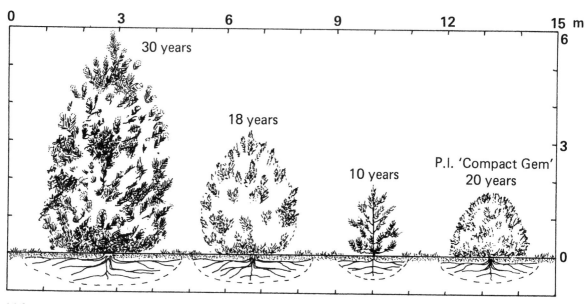

Plant associations   The dwarf and tall forms look well among other evergreens, or with dwarf shrubs, heathers or rock plants.

Pest and disease control   Control adelges by spraying with HCH, repeating the following year in spring as a preventive measure. Spring sprays of HCH should also prevent attacks of Pine shoot moth caterpillars. Sawfly larvae can be controlled by sprays of fenitrothion or malathion. To check canker and dieback cut out affected areas and spray with a copper fungicide. If planting on land which may have been contaminated with honey fungus, first remove all old tree stumps and sterilize the soil with formaldehyde. Allow four to six weeks for the formaldehyde fumes to dissipate from the soil before planting. Rusts can be checked by spraying with a copper or thiram fungicide.

Propagation   By seed sown in spring. Named varieties by grafting in spring.

Season of interest	Winter	Spring	Late spring	Summer	Late summer	Autumn
In full leaf	X—					—X
Autumn colour						
Flowers						
Fruits				X—		—X
Bark and stem						

The following five characteristics determine to a great extent the amount of attention a specific tree requires.

	When planted	5 years	20 years
Height	600 mm	1·5 m	4·0 m
Width	450 mm	1·0 m	3·0 m
Root spread	450 mm	1·5 m	4·0 m
Hardiness	C	B	A/B
Wind-firm	3	2	1

Plant care profile

	Minimum Average High
Site needs	X——X
Soil needs	X
Pruning	X——X
Staking	X
Maintenance	X——X

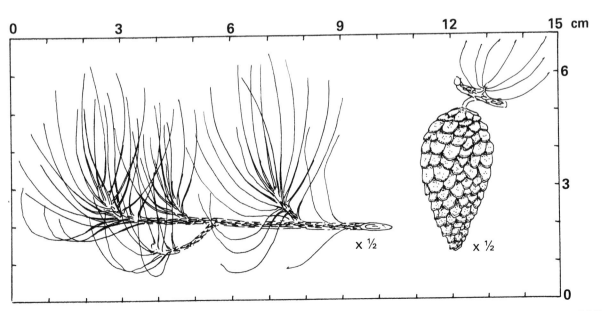

x ½   x ½

Pinus mugo – PINACEAE
Mountain Pine

A very hardy evergreen tree or shrub.
Origin Europe.

Uses
The Mountain Pine is admirable as an individual specimen, in mixed plantings, and as ground cover.

Description
Dimensions Exceptionally variable. Garden forms vary in both height and width from about 1.5m (5ft) to 4.5m (15ft). In the natural state the variation is even greater.
Rate of growth Usually slow.
Life span Like the dimensions, very indefinite, but these Pines can be expected to live a minimum of 30 years.
Habit Bushy and spreading.
Leaves Mid-green and needle-like, usually arranged in pairs. The buds at the tips of shoots are brownish and resinous.
Flowers Inconspicuous.
Fruits Brown cones, up to 60mm (2½in.) long.
Bark Concealed by branches as a rule. Usually hidden by dense foliage.

Features
The Mountain Pine is less demanding than many conifers as regards site and soil, and it can be successfully grown where less accommodating plants would fail.
Polluion Tolerant.
Non-poisonous.

Varieties
Pinus mugo 'Gnom'. A compact rounded dwarf conifer. Ultimate height and spread rarely exceeds 1.5–1.8m (5–6ft). Foliage mid- to dark green.
Pinus mugo pumilio. A compact form which can reach an ultimate height and spread 1.5–2m (5–7ft). A bushy habit with several stems rising from ground level. Foliage dark blue-green. Tolerates poor, dry soils.

Requirements
Position A mild or cool temperate climate suits this Pine, which grows naturally near the highest limits of vegetation on mountains in central Europe. It needs an open situation in full sun, preferably not too exposed to strong prevailing winds.

Soil A well drained loam that is acid to slightly acid, pH 6–6.5, is ideal, but the Mountain Pine and its varieties can grow successfully on poor, dry soils once they are established. On poor soils apply a dressing of 70g per sq. m (2oz. per sq. yd) of general fertilizer before planting, and repeat each spring.

Notes on culture
Planting Plant small conifers, up to 450mm (1½ft) high, in autumn, winter or spring. Staking and tying is not necessary.
Space Allow each plant a minimum area of about 1.8m (6ft) diameter at maturity. Where groups of two or more of the same type are planted together the distance between can be reduced to 1.2m (4ft). Avoid planting closer to buildings than 1.8m (6ft).
Pruning Cut back any damaged, diseased or untidy shoots to maintain a good shape. This should be done late spring.
Plant associations These trees look well when planted in groups with other conifers, or with shrubs and heathers, and are excellent as shelter for alpines and rock plants.

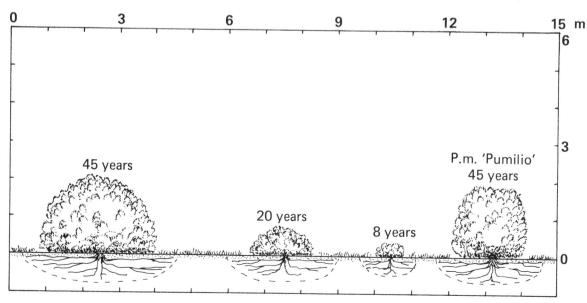

Pest and disease control Control adelges by spraying with HCH, repeating the following year in spring as a preventive measure. Spring sprays of HCH should also prevent attacks of Pine shoot moth caterpillar. Sawfly larvae can be controlled by sprays of fenitrothion or malathion. If planting on land which may have been contaminated with honey fungus, first remove all old tree stumps and sterilize the soil with formaldehyde. Allow four to six weeks for the formaldehyde fumes to dissipate from the soil before planting. Rusts can be checked by spraying with a copper or thiram fungicide.

Propagation By seed sown in spring. Named varieties or special selections by grafting in spring.

Season of interest	Winter	Spring	Late spring	Summer	Late summer	Autumn
In full leaf	X—————					—————X
Autumn colour						
Flowers						
Fruits					X—————	—————X
Bark and stem	———X				X—————	

The following five characteristics determine to a great extent the amount of attention a specific tree requires.

	When planted	5 years	20 years
Height	450 mm	700 mm	1·2 m
Width	450 mm	900 mm	2·0 m
Root spread	450 mm	1·0 m	2·5 m
Hardiness	C	B	A/B
Wind-firm	2	1	1

Plant care profile

	Minimum	Average	High
Site needs		X	
Soil needs		X	
Pruning	X		
Staking	X		
Maintenance	X—————	—X	

Size at 20 years refers to dwarf type.

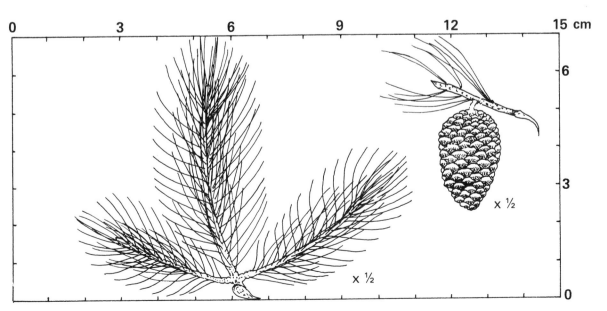

x ½

x ½

119

Pinus nigra – PINACEAE
Austrian Pine

A hardy evergreen tree or shrub.
Origin Europe.

Uses
The tall Pine makes a handsome specimen and where space allows can be used for shelter and screening. Dwarf varieties are ideal for planting singly or in groups, in rock gardens or in containers.

Description
Dimensions Ultimate size infrequently exceeds 10.5m (35ft) high by 6–7.5m (20–25ft) wide, but under ideal conditions in a warm summer climate trees can grow to double this size.
Rate of growth Moderate to rapid in the early stages, slowing down later.
Life span Variable, but these conifers can live 70 years and more.
Habit Usually columnar or pyramidal, becoming flat-topped in maturity.
Leaves Mid- to dark grey-green, and arranged in pairs.
Flowers Inconspicuous.
Fruits Roughly conical or ovoid cones, usually brown when ripe, 50–75mm (2–3in.) long, and occurring in groups of two or three.

Bark Dark grey and deeply furrowed.

Features
This Pine is hardy, root- and wind-firm, and can safely withstand cold and exposed situations as well as some inferior soils.
Pollution Tolerant.
Non-poisonous.

Varieties
Pinus nigra 'Hornibrookiana'. A bushy, compact conifer, ultimately about 1.5–1.8m (5–6ft) high by the same wide. Dark green foliage.
Pinus nigra maritima (Corsican Pine). A large, strong-growing tree which reaches about 13.5m (45ft) high by 7.5m (25ft) wide. The trunk is longer and straighter than that of the true Austrian Pine. Unfortunately, this Pine does not transplant well once past the seedling stage. Mainly used for forestry purposes.
Pinus nigra 'Pygmaea'. A bushy dwarf conifer eventually growing to about 2–2.5m (7–8ft) high by the same width. Green, slightly twisted leaves which turn a pleasant yellow during winter.

Requirements
Position These Pines grow best in mild temperate climates with warm summers. Open, sunny situations in full light are most suitable. They can tolerate drier conditions than many conifers.
Soil A well drained loam that is slightly acid, pH 6.5, is ideal, but these conifers can grow on neutral or chalky ground, even on soils that are dry and poor. On poor soils apply a dressing of 70g per sq. m (2oz. per sq. yd) of general fertilizer before planting, and repeat each spring.

Notes on culture
Planting Plant small conifers, not more than 300m (1ft) high. Autumn is the best time for planting, but plants can also be moved during winter and spring when conditions allow. Staking and tying is not necessary. Keep the ground weed-free and mulched within a 600mm (2ft) radius of young plants.
Space Allow each tree or shrub a minimum area equal in diameter to its width at maturity and similar distance from buildings. Temporary plantings may be made closer to

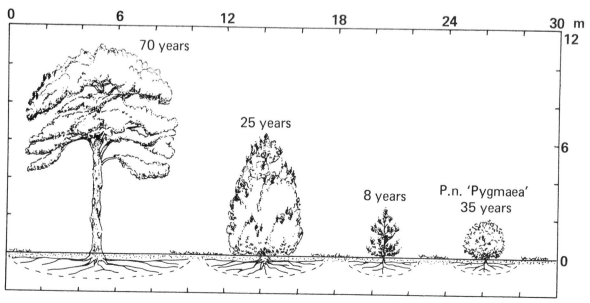

0   6   12   18   24   30 m

70 years

25 years

8 years

P.n. 'Pygmaea'
35 years

young Pines, but filler plants must be removed in good time to prevent overcrowding.

Pruning Prune tree forms to limit main shoots to one central leader. On all types cut back any damaged, diseased or untidy shoots to maintain a good shape. All pruning should be done in late spring.

Plant associations Effective when planted with conifers of different or contrasting form and outline.

Pest and disease control Control adelges by spraying with HCH, repeating the following year in spring as a preventive measure. Spring sprays of HCH should also prevent attacks of Pine shoot moth caterpillars. Sawfly larvae can be controlled by sprays of fenitrothion or malathion. If planting on land which may have been contaminated with honey fungus, first remove all old tree stumps and sterilize the soil with formaldehyde. Allow four to six weeks for the formaldehyde fumes to dissipate from the soil before planting. Rusts can be checked by spraying with a copper or thiram fungicide.

Propagation By seed sown in spring. Named varieties by grafting in spring.

Season of interest	Winter	Spring	Late spring	Summer	Late summer	Autumn
In full leaf	X————	———	———	———	———	—X
Autumn colour						
Flowers			X—	—X		
Fruits						
Bark and stem	X——	——	——	——	——	—X

The following five characteristics determine to a great extent the amount of attention a specific tree requires.

	When planted	5 years	20 years
Height	300mm	1·8m	6·0m
Width	100mm	1·2m	4·0m
Root spread	100mm	1·5m	5·0m
Hardiness	B/C	B	A/B
Wind-firm	3	2	1

Plant care profile

	Minimum Average High
Site needs	X
Soil needs	X
Pruning	X——X
Staking	X
Maintenance	X——X

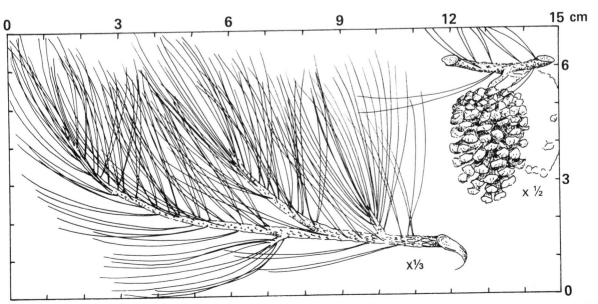

x ½

x ⅓

121

Pinus parviflora – PINACEAE
Japanese White Pine

A moderately hardy evergreen tree.
Origin Japan.

Uses
The Japanese White Pine and its varieties make fine specimen trees for large and medium gardens.

Description
Dimensions Trees can reach an ultimate size of 7.5–9m (25–30ft) high by 4–4.5m (13–15ft) wide, but smaller trees than this are usual.
Rate of growth Moderate to slow.
Life span Trees can be expected to grow for 40–50 years or more before starting to decline.
Habit Columnar or pyramidal, with a low crown of thickly set, wide-spreading branches.
Leaves Needle-like, 40–60mm (1½–2½in.) long, arranged in groups of five, and varying in colour from blue-green to greyish green.
Flowers Inconspicuous.
Fruits Brown, oval cones, 50–100mm (2–4in.) long, and usually produced three or four together in considerable numbers. They often persist for several years on the tree.
Bark Purple, with dark grey or black scales.

Features
The neat growth and comparatively small size of the Japanese White Pine have made this species popular.
Pollution Fairly tolerant.
Non-poisonous.

Variety
Pinus parviflora 'Adcocks Dwarf' and *Pinus parviflora* 'Brevifolia' are both dwarf rounded forms reaching about 1.5m (5ft) in height.
Pinus parviflora 'Glauca'. Narrower in habit, more upright and less dense than the species when young. Approximate ultimate size 7–9m (23–30ft) high by 3–4m (10–13ft) wide. Foliage a glaucous blue-green.

Requirements
Position A sunny, open situation, preferably protected from strong prevailing winds, in an area with a mild or cool temperate climate suits these trees.
Soil A well drained but moist, light to medium loam that is acid to slightly acid pH 6–6.5, is most suitable.

Notes on culture .
Planting Plant small trees, up to 600mm (2ft) high. Autumn is the best time for planting, but these trees can also be moved during winter and spring. Staking and tying is not necessary.
Space Allow a minimum area of 4.5m (15ft) diameter at maturity, and avoid planting closer to buildings than 6m (20ft).
Pruning If the leading shoot is damaged or ceases to grow cut back to sound wood, train one shoot from the whorl immediately below, and remove the remainder. Otherwise the less cutting the better, apart from removing any damaged, diseased or untidy shoots. All pruning should be done in late spring.
Plant associations This Pine and varieties look well with rhododendrons and heathers.

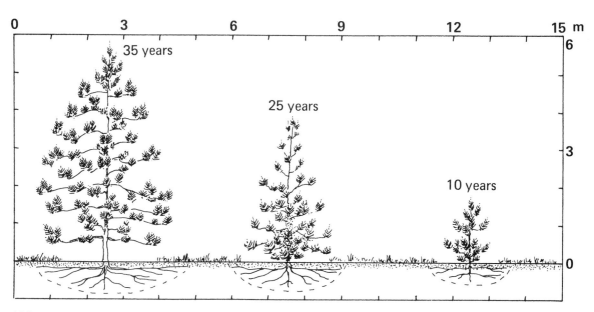

Pest and disease control Control adelges by spraying with HCH, repeating the following year in spring as a preventive measure. Spring sprays of HCH should also prevent attacks of Pine shoot moth caterpillars. Sawfly larvae can be controlled by sprays of fenitrothion or malathion. If planting on land which may have been contaminated with honey fungus, first remove all old tree stumps and sterilize the soil with formaldehyde. Allow four to six weeks for the formaldehyde fumes to dissipate from the soil before planting.
Propagation By seed sown in spring. Named varieties by grafting in spring.

Season of interest	Winter	Spring	Late spring	Summer	Late summer	Autumn
In full leaf	X———	———	———	———	———	——X
Autumn colour						
Flowers						
Fruits			———X	X———	———	———
Bark and stem	X———	———	———	———	———	——X

The following five characteristics determine to a great extent the amount of attention a specific tree requires.

	When planted	5 years	20 years
Height	600 mm	1·0 m	4·0 m
Width	300 mm	650 mm	2·5 m
Root spread	300 mm	1·0 m	3·5 m
Hardiness	C	C	B/C
Wind-firm	3	2/3	2

Plant care profile

	Minimum Average High
Site needs	X————X
Soil needs	X
Pruning	X————X
Staking	X
Maintenance	X————X

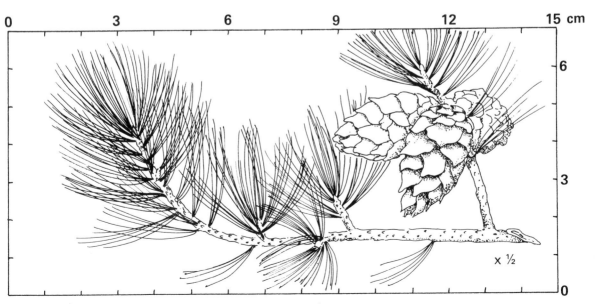

0   3   6   9   12   15 cm

x ½

Pinus sylvestris – PINACEAE
Scots Pine, Scotch Pine

A very hardy evergreen tree.
Origin Asia and Europe.

Uses
The Scots Pine is effective as a single specimen or when planted in groups. The dwarf conifers are excellent alone or in mixed plantings, in beds or in rock gardens.

Description
Dimensions Average ultimate size 12m (40ft) high by 5m (17ft) wide, but can grow half as tall again in good conditions.
Rate of growth Slow to moderate.
Life span Under good conditions these conifers can live for 70 years or more.
Habit Pyramidal when young, becoming flat-topped or irregular and exposing the trunk as lower branches progress beyond their useful life.
Leaves Grey-green and arranged in pairs.
Flowers Inconspicuous.
Fruits Pale brown cones, usually 40–50mm (1½–2in.) long, borne at the tips of shoots or branches on trees 10 years old and over.
Bark A very distinctive reddish brown, forming fissures on older trees.

Features
Form a rugged flat-topped tree when mature, with distinctive bark and characteristic outline. Very hardy and wind-firm.
Pollution Tolerant.
Non-poisonous.

Varieties
Pinus sylvestris 'Aurea'. A slow-growing tree, columnar in outline, and only occasionally exceeding 5–6m (17–20ft) high. Summer foliage green, turning yellow in winter.
Pinus sylvestris 'Beuvronensis'. An attractive bushy form which can grow to an ultimate size of 900m (3ft) high by 1.2m (4ft) wide. Foliage mid-green with prominent winter buds.
Pinus sylvestris 'Fastigiata'. A narrowly upright pyramidal form, slower-growing than the species.
Pinus sylvestris 'Pygmaea'. A rounded form reaching 1.8m (6ft) high.
Pinus sylvestris 'Watereri'. A form which is pyramidal when young becoming more rounded with age. Average ultimate size 5–6m (17–20ft) high by about the same wide.

Requirements
Position A sunny or lightly shaded situation in a cool temperate climate suits these Pines. The species can tolerate exposed sites, but the varieties, especially *P.s.* 'Aurea', are better when protected from severe cold or drying winds.
Soil A moist but well drained loam that is slightly acid, pH 6.5, is ideal, but the Scots Pine can tolerate neutral or chalk soils, as well as more acid conditions. On poor or sandy soils apply a dressing of 70g per sq. m (2oz. per sq. yd) of general fertilizer before planting, and repeat each spring.

Notes on culture
Planting Plant seedlings or young plants, up to 600mm (2ft) high. Autumn is the best time for planting, but these Pines can also be moved during winter and spring. Staking and tying is not necessary.
Space Allow each tree or shrub a minimum area equal in diameter to its width at maturity, and avoid planting the species closer to buildings than 6m (20ft).
Pruning Tree forms of this Pine are crown-lifted, that is, have the lower branches removed to expose the bark to view. If the leading shoot is damaged or ceases to grow,

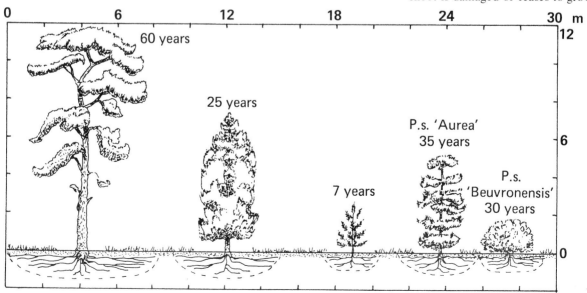

60 years

25 years

P.s. 'Aurea'
35 years

7 years

P.s. 'Beuvronensis'
30 years

cut back to sound wood, train one shoot from the whorl immediately below, and remove the remainder. Bush forms need no pruning apart from removing any damaged, diseased or untidy shoots to maintain a good shape. Pruning is carried out in late spring.

Plant associations On acid soils tree forms may effectively be underplanted with rhododendrons. The dwarf varieties look very well among other dwarf conifers.

Pest and disease control Control adelges by spraying with HCH, repeating the following year in spring as a preventive measure. Spring sprays of HCH should also prevent attacks of Pine shoot moth caterpillars. Sawfly larvae can be controlled by sprays of fenitrothion or malathion. If planting on land which may have been contaminated with honey fungus, first remove all old tree stumps and sterilize the soil with formaldehyde. Allow four to six weeks for the formaldehyde fumes to dissipate from the soil before planting. Rusts can be checked by spraying with a copper or thiram fungicide.

Propagation By seed sown in spring. Named varieties by grafting in spring.

Season of interest	Winter	Spring	Late spring	Summer	Late summer	Autumn
In full leaf	X———————————————————————————X					
Autumn colour						
Flowers						
Fruits				X—	X———————	
Bark and stem	X———————————————————————————X					

The following five characteristics determine to a great extent the amount of attention a specific tree requires.

	When planted	5 years	20 years
Height	600 mm	2·5 m	6·5 m
Width	250 mm	1·5 m	3·0 m
Root spread	250 mm	2·5 m	4·5 m
Hardiness	B	A	A
Wind-firm	2	1	1

Plant care profile

	Minimum	Average	High
Site needs		X———X	
Soil needs		X	
Pruning	X———X		
Staking	X		
Maintenance	X———X		

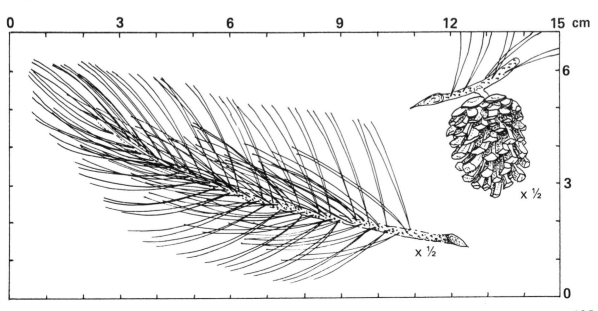

x ½

x ½

Pseudotsuga menziesii – PINACEAE
Douglas Fir

A hardy evergreen tree.
Origin Asia and USA.

Uses
The true Douglas Fir is too big and vigorous for any but the largest garden. However, there are some varieties which are very useful in gardens. *P.m. glauca* can make a very imposing specimen in a large or medium garden. The dwarf type can be used in gardens of almost any size. It is very effective as a specimen or in mixed plantings, in beds, or rock gardens.

Description
Dimensions Variable, ultimate size ranges from 10.5 to 23m (35 to 75ft) high, from 4.5 to 6m (15 to 20ft) wide.
Rate of growth Rapid.
Life span In good conditions trees can live for 100 years or more.
Habit Narrowly pyramidal and spire-like when young, gradually developing a broad, flattish crown.
Leaves Needle-like, with dark green upper surface and pale reverse. The foliage is usually fairly thick and soft, and has an aromatic scent when crushed.
Flowers The male flowers are insignificant clusters of pinkish stamens. Reddish female flowers.

Fruits Soft but weedy cones, with three-pronged bracts between the scales. They normally develop and mature the first season after flowering, on trees which are 10 years old and over.
Bark On older trees dark brown, blistered, deeply furrowed and corky. Young bark is dark grey.

Features
The species makes a very large tree, unlike the varieties which are excellent for garden use. These are hardy and wind-firm, requiring little attention.
Pollution Fairly tolerant.
Non-poisonous.

Varieties
Pseudotsuga menziesii 'Fletcheri'. An outstanding dwarf conifer of bushy habit. Can reach an ultimate size of 900mm–1.2m (3–4ft) high by 1.2–1.5m (4–5ft) wide. Foliage a glaucous blue-green.
Pseudotsuga menziesii glauca. Slower-growing and smaller than the species, rarely exceeding 10.5 (35ft) high by 3m (10ft) wide. Blue-grey foliage. Grows better on poor, dry soils than the species.

Requirements
Position A region with a mild or cool temperate climate suits these trees. The species does best in an area of high rainfall. The varieties grow well in sunny or lightly shaded situations that are sheltered from cold or hot drying winds, and they can tolerate drier conditions than the true Douglas Fir.
Soil A deep, fertile, well drained, medium loam that is slightly acid, pH 6.5, is most suitable.

Notes on culture
Planting Plant small trees, up to about 450mm (1½ft) high. Spring is the best time for planting, but trees can also be successfully moved in autumn. Staking and tying is not necessary for small trees. Keep the ground around young plants weed-free, well watered and mulched.
Space The species is too strong-growing for most gardens, but not so the varieties. Allow a minimum area of 4m (13ft) diameter at maturity for *P.m. glauca*, 1.5m (5ft) for *P.m.* 'Fletcheri'. Avoid placing the larger variety closer to buildings than 7.5m (25ft).

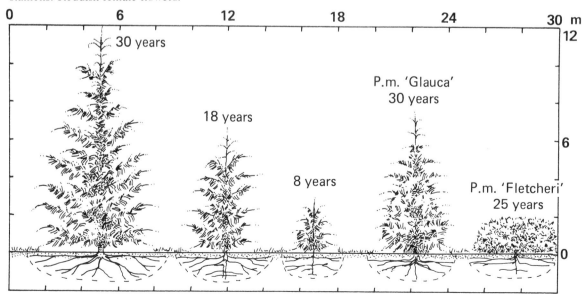

Pruning Prune to limit main shoots to one central leader, and cut back any damaged, diseased or untidy shoots to maintain a good shape. All pruning should be done in late spring.

Plant associations The species and variety *P.m. glauca* are effective when grown in grass. The dwarf variety may be planted among other dwarf conifers or with rock plants.

Pest and disease control Adelges, apparent by their wool-like tufts and pineapple-like galls, can seriously weaken young trees, and should be checked with HCH sprays. Trees are not greatly troubled by diseases after the planting-out stage, but seedlings may be attacked by grey mould or botrytis. Remove affected seedlings and spray with a benomyl or thiram fungicide.

Propagation The species and *P.m glauca* by seed sown in spring. Other named varieties usually by grafting in spring.

Season of interest	Winter	Spring	Late spring	Summer	Late summer	Autumn
In full leaf	X———	———	———	———	———	———X
Autumn colour						
Flowers						
Fruits				X———	———	———X
Bark and stem						

The following five characteristics determine to a great extent the amount of attention a specific tree requires.

	When planted	5 years	20 years
Height	450mm	2·0 m	7·5 m
Width	200mm	1·2 m	2·0 m
Root spread	200mm	2·0 m	3·0 m
Hardiness	C	B	A/B
Wind-firm	3	2	1/2

Plant care profile

	Minimum	Average	High
Site needs		X———X	
Soil needs		X———X	
Pruning	X———X		
Staking	X———X		
Maintenance		X	

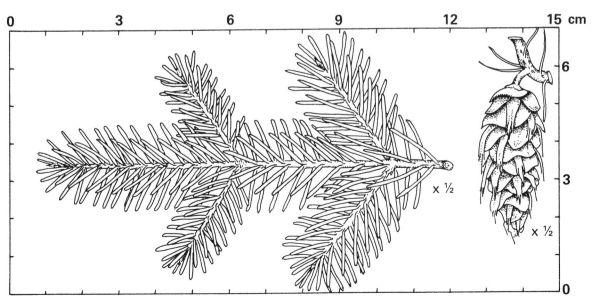

x ½

x ½

Taxodium distichum – TAXODIACEAE
Deciduous Cypress, Swamp Cypress

A moderately hardy deciduous tree.
Origin   USA.

Uses
The Swamp Cypress and its
varieties are best suited to large
and medium gardens. They lend
themselves to waterside planting in
particular.

Description
Dimensions   Ultimate size rarely
exceeds 12m (40ft) high by 5m
(17ft) wide.
Rate of growth   Usually slow.
Life span   Trees can grow for
considerably more than 100 years.
Habit   Typically narrow and
pyramidal when young, tapering
slightly to the top; broadens out
with age.
Leaves   New season's leaves a light
yellowish green, turning in autumn
to reddish brown and russet shades
and becoming brown just before
the leaves fall.
Flowers   Male catkins, purplish
and 100–150mm (4–6in.) long,
appear before the trees are in leaf.
Female flowers are insignificant.
Fruits   Mid-brown cones, but these
occur only infrequently.

Bark   Reddish brown with shallow
furrows. The branch stems are
orange-brown, but the tips are
grey-green in early summer.

Features
The Swamp Cypress is a fairly
accommodating tree, presenting few
problems, and is root- and
wind-firm. The autumn foliage can
be quite colourful especially where
reflected on water.
Pollution   Tolerant.
Non-poisonous.

Variety
Taxodium distichum 'Pendens'.
Branch tips pendant, arching
downwards.

Requirements
Position   A mild or warm
temperate climate suits these trees.
Both sunny and shaded situations
are suitable, but shelter from strong
or cold winds is necessary, and
young seedlings, which are not
frost-hardy, require protection in
hard weather.

Soil   A fertile, moist soil that is
acid, pH 6, produces the best
results, but the Swamp Cypress will
tolerate alkaline soils. Trees
planted on thin, gravelly soils can
grow successfully provided the
roots are kept wet or moist at all
times. Avoid stagnant conditions,
but trees can and do grow well in
shallow water.

Notes on culture
Planting   Plant small trees,
600–900mm (2–3ft) high. Late
spring is the best time for planting,
but plants can be set out in autumn
if young trees are protected from
severe frost during winter. Staking
and tying is not necessary for small
plants, but larger trees need
support until firmly rooted.
Space   Allow a minimum area of
5m (17ft) diameter at maturity.
Avoid planting closer to buildings
than 7.5m (25ft), especially on clay
soils, as the drying effect of trees
on the subsoil can seriously damage
foundations.

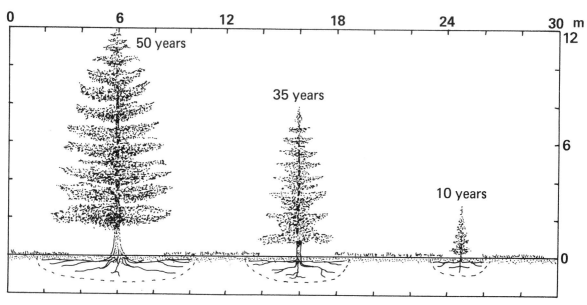

Pruning Prune in spring to limit main shoots to one central leader, and cut back any damaged or diseased shoots. Otherwise little or no cutting is necessary.

Plant associations The Swamp Cypress and waterside plants make a pleasing combination. Large-leaved Gunneras contrast effectively with the feathery foliage of this tree.

Pest and disease control Rarely necessary.

Propagation By seed sown in mid- to late spring.

Season of interest	Winter	Spring	Late spring	Summer	Late summer	Autumn
In full leaf			X————		—X	
Autumn colour					X——	—X
Flowers						
Fruits						
Bark and stem	X——					—X

The following five characteristics determine to a great extent the amount of attention a specific tree requires.

	When planted	5 years	20 years
Height	750 mm	1·5 m	6·0 m
Width	250 mm	500 mm	2·0 m
Root spread	250 mm	1·0 m	3·0 m
Hardiness	C	C	B/C
Wind-firm	3	2	1/2

Plant care profile

	Minimum Average High
Site needs	X————X
Soil needs	X
Pruning	X————X
Staking	X
Maintenance	X————X

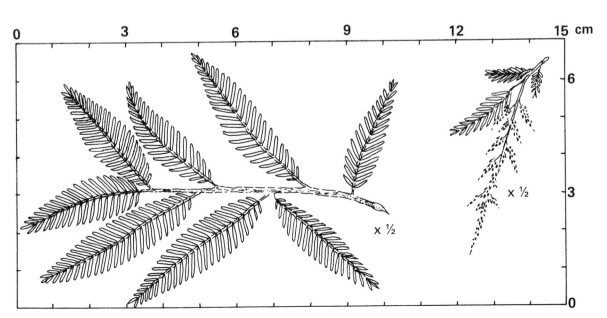

x ½

x ½

129

Taxus baccata – TAXACEAE
Common Yew, English Yew

A very hardy small tree or shrub.
Origin Asia, Europe and northern Africa.

Uses
Upright varieties, such as the green or golden Irish Yew, make excellent single specimens, or look very well in a pair, on either side of an entrance. Yews may also be planted in groups, for hedging or ground cover.

Description
Dimensions Variable, but ultimate size rarely exceeds 6m (20ft) high by the same wide.
Rate of growth Moderate for the first few years, then slow.
Life span The Common Yew is one of the longest-lived plants grown in gardens. Yew trees over 400 years are known.
Habit Much-branched, with vertical and horizontal main branches.
Leaves Needle-like, with dark green upper surface and yellowish green reverse.
Flowers Flowers of opposite sexes are usually carried on separate plants. The male flowers, which are pale yellow, can be seen in late spring on the underside of the foliage. The female flowers, carried singly are inconspicuous.
Fruits Red, fleshy, cup-shaped fruits about 6–8mm (¼–⅓ in.) across.
Bark Usually reddish brown and scaly.

Features
The Yew is very hardy, root- and wind-firm. Its one disadvantage is that the foliage is poisonous; it should never be planted where grazing animals could eat the leaves. The berries are not poisonous.
Pollution Resistant.
Poisonous.

Varieties
Taxus baccata 'Adpressa Variegata'. Very slow-growing, but ultimately can reach 1.5–1.8m (5–6ft) high by 900mm–1.2m (3–4ft) wide. Foliage yellow, old leaves having a central green stripe.
Taxus baccata 'Dovastoniana'. Upright stem with horizontal branches, green leaves. Height and spread as type.
Taxus baccata 'Fastigiata' (Irish Yew). A form with an upright columnar habit. Ultimate size 3–4m (10–13ft) by one-quarter to one-third as wide. Foliage dark green, slow-growing.
Taxus baccata 'Fastigiata Aureomarginata'. A golden-leaved form of the Irish Yew.
Taxus baccata 'Repandans'. A low-growing form which is dark green and suitable for ground cover. Slow-growing, reaching ultimately about 450mm (1½ft) high by 2.5–3m (8–10ft) wide.
Taxus baccata 'Semperaurea'. A very fine golden Yew, retaining its colour well. This Yew rarely exceeds 1.5–2m (5–7ft) high by 1.8–2.5m (6–8ft) wide.

Requirements
Position Mild or cool temperate climates both support good growth. Sunny or lightly shaded situations are suitable for varieties with green leaves, but full sun is best for variegated kinds. Although open or exposed sites are tolerated, growth is faster in more sheltered spots.
Soil A well drained but moist loam that is neutral to slightly alkaline, pH 7–7.3 is ideal, but these Yews can be grown successfully in a wide range of soil types: peaty, gravelly, sandy land, shallow ground over chalk or limestone, dry land. Badly drained ground, however, is not suitable.

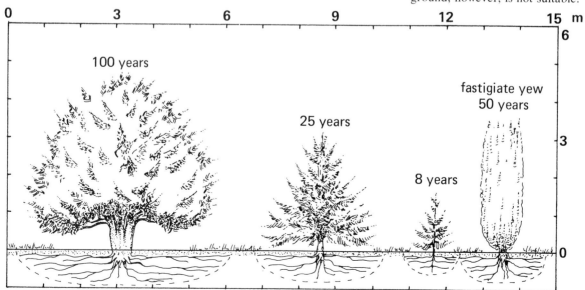

100 years

25 years

fastigiate yew 50 years

8 years

Notes on culture

Planting Plant small conifers, 300–600mm (1–2ft) high, in autumn, winter or spring. Staking and tying is unneccessary. Keep the ground around young plants weed-free and well watered.

Space Most Yews can be clipped to contain them within confined areas, but spreading kinds, such as *T.b.* 'Dovastoniana', being less amenable to cutting, need a minimum area of 3–4m (10–13ft) diameter at maturity. With the exception of the spreading varieties, Yews can be planted to within 1.2m (4ft) of buildings.

Pruning Little or none need be done beyond removing misplaced or surplus shoots. However, Yews can stand regular trimming, hence their former wide use in topiary work. Pruning should be done in late spring.

Plant associations Yews are particularly effective as a background for a bold display of flowers.

Pest and disease control The problem most likely to be met with is Yew scale, appearing as oval brown scales on stems and foliage. Severe outbreaks weaken trees and cause loss of leaves. It can be controlled by a tar oil spray in mid-winter and diazinon or malathion sprays at other times of the year, repeating the application as necessary.

Propagation By seed sown in autumn. Variegated and named varieties by cuttings taken in late summer or early autumn.

Season of interest	Winter	Spring	Late spring	Summer	Late summer	Autumn
In full leaf	X———					——X
Autumn colour						
Flowers			X—X			
Fruits						
Bark and stem	X———					——X

The following five characteristics determine to a great extent the amount of attention a specific tree requires.

	When planted	5 years	20 years
Height	600 mm	1·0 m	3·0 m
Width	450 mm	1·0 m	3·0 m
Root spread	450 mm	1·5 m	4·0 m
Hardiness	B	A	A
Wind-firm	2	1	1

Plant care profile

	Minimum	Average	High
Site needs			X
Soil needs			X
Pruning	X———	———X	
Staking	X		
Maintenance			X

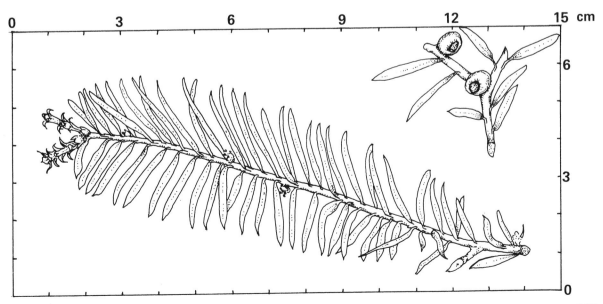

131

Thuja occidentalis – CUPRESSACEAE
American Arbor-vitae, White Cedar

A moderately hardy evergreen tree.
Origin Canada and eastern north USA.

Uses
The true White Cedar can be used as a specimen tree, but it is really only suitable for large gardens. The varieties are excellent when used as single specimens. The dwarf conifers look well in groups or mixed plantings, in beds or rock gardens. They can also be used to good effect when planted in containers, tubs and troughs.

Description
Dimensions Ultimate size occasionally exceeds 7.5–9m (25–30ft) high by 5m (17ft) wide in gardens, but can double these dimensions in good conditions.
Rate of growth Slow to moderate.
Life span Variable, but trees start to decline at about 30 years old.
Habit Pyramidal when young, becoming more open and irregular with age.
Leaves Scale-like and flattish, with mid-green upper surface and yellowish grey-green reverse. The foliage is arranged in curled sprays which hang down and give off an acrid smell when crushed.

Flowers Inconspicuous.
Fruits Cones which are yellowish at first, later turning brown, and about 8mm (1/3 in.) long.
Bark Brownish-grey, but usually covered by foliage.

Features
Although the type species is planted only to a limited extent, there are a number of fine varieties which have arisen from it.
Pollution Fairly tolerant.
Non-poisonous.

Varieties
Thuja occidentalis 'Aurea'. A golden-leaved form, less vigorous than the species.
Thuja occidentalis 'Hetz' Midget'. A slow-growing dwarf conifer with mid- to dark green foliage. Ultimate size approximately 600mm (2ft) high by the same wide.
Thuja occidentalis 'Holmstrupii'. A small, neat conifer ultimately reaching about 3–3.5m (10–12ft) high by 1.5–1.8m (5–6ft) wide. Foliage deep green through the year.
Thuja occidentalis 'Lutea'. Strong growing with golden foliage and pyramidal habit. Similar size to species.

Thuja occidentalis 'Lutea Nana'. A golden yellow slow-growing globose form, reaching 1.8m (6ft) high. Foliage colour retained year round.
Thuja occidentalis 'Rheingold'. Slow-growing dwarf and conical in habit. Occasionally reaches 2.5m (8ft) high by about the same wide. Leaves golden in summer turning coppery yellow in autumn.
Thuja occidentalis 'Spiralis'. A narrow pyramidal form with deep green foliage. Ultimate size approximately 4–5m (13–17ft) high by 1.8–2m (6–7ft) wide.

Requirements
Position A sunny but sheltered situation, well protected from strong and freezing winds, in an area with a moist warm or mild temperate climate, suits these trees. Golden forms especially should be placed in full sun.
Soil A deep, well drained but moist, light to medium loam that is slightly acid, pH 6.5 or near, is most suitable. On poor or sandy soils apply a dressing of 70g per sq. m (2oz. per sq. yd.) of general fertilizer before planting, and repeat each spring for the first few years.

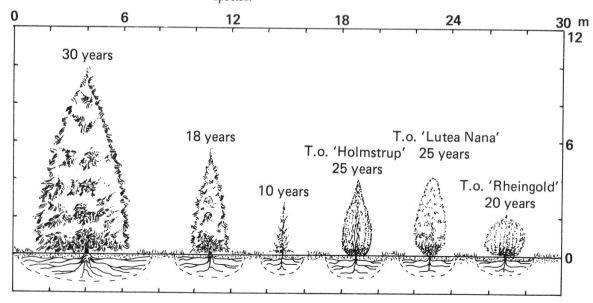

Notes on culture

Planting Plant small trees, up to 600mm (2ft) high, in autumn or late spring, or, if weather permits, in winter. Staking and tying is not necessary for small plants. Keep the ground around young plants weed-free, well watered and mulched.

Space Allow each tree a minimum area equal in diameter to its width at maturity. Avoid planting the species closer to buildings than about 6–7.5m (20–25ft).

Pruning Cut back any damaged, diseased or untidy shoots to maintain a good shape. This should be done in late spring.

Plant associations The dwarf and tall conifers look effective among other evergreens, or planted around with dwarf shrubs, heathers or rock plants.

Pest and disease control Rarely necessary.

Propagation By seed sown in spring. Special forms and named varieties by cuttings taken in late summer or early autumn.

Season of interest	Winter	Spring	Late spring	Summer	Late summer	Autumn
In full leaf	X—					—X
Autumn colour						
Flowers						
Fruits	——		X	X—		
Bark and stem						

The following five characteristics determine to a great extent the amount of attention a specific tree requires.

	When planted	5 years	20 years
Height	600 mm	1·8 m	6·0m
Width	200 mm	600mm	1·8 m
Root spread	200 mm	1·0m	2·5 m
Hardiness	C	C	B/C
Wind-firm	3	2/3	2

Plant care profile

	Minimum	Average	High
Site needs		X——X	
Soil needs		X	
Pruning		X	
Staking	X		
Maintenance		X	

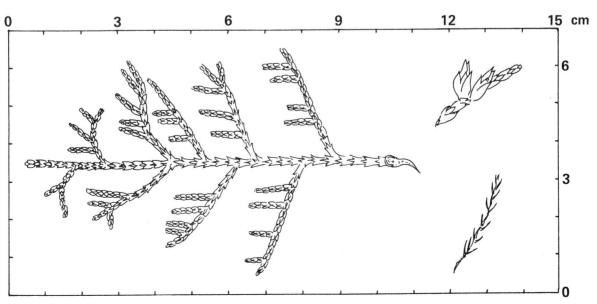

Thuja orientalis – CUPRESSACEAE
Chinese Arbor-vitae, Oriental Arbor-vitae

A moderately hardy evergreen small tree or shrub.
Origin   China.

Uses

The Chinese Arbor-vitae and its varieties can be very effective when used as single specimens. The small conifers lend themselves well to being planted in rock gardens. They can be grown in containers, but their dislike of dry conditions makes them less suitable for this than some of the other kinds of dwarf conifer.

Description

Dimensions   Average ultimate size 6m (20ft) high by 3–3.5m (10–12ft) wide.
Rate of growth   Usually slow.
Life span   Variable, but these conifers usually start to decline at between 30 and 40 years old.
Habit   There are two distinct types of habit: one is pyramidal and sparsely covered; the other rounded or oval in outline and shrubby in character, with fairly dense foliage. These two forms are similar in other respects.

Leaves   Scale-like, mid-green in summer, becoming bronze-green in winter, and arranged collectively to form vertical flat branches.
Flowers   Insignificant.
Fruits   Pale brown cones about 18mm (¾in.) long.
Bark   Dark grey, but, as a rule, well hidden by foliage.

Features

The pyramidal and oval forms have very distinctive foliage arranged vertically in plate form. Moderately hardy.
Pollution   Fairly tolerant.
Non-poisonous.

Varieties

Thuja orientalis 'Aurea Nana'. A dwarf conifer of upright oval habit. Rarely grows to more than 900mm–1.2m (3–4ft) high by 750mm –1m(2½–3½ft) wide. Foliage golden yellow in summer, bronze-green in winter.
Thuja orientalis 'Elegantissima'. A slow-growing upright form with conical top. Eventually reaches 2.5–3m (8–10ft) high by 900mm–1.2m (3–4ft) wide. Foliage golden in summer, bronze in winter.

Thuja orientalis 'Rosedalis'. A very slow-growing dwarf conifer which can reach an ultimate size of 600–900mm (2–3ft) high by about the same wide. The foliage, which, unlike that of the species *T. orientalis* and the other varieties, retains the juvenile form, is light green in summer, turning to shades of purple in winter.

Requirements

Position   A sunny but sheltered situation in an area with a moist mild temperate climate suits those plants. They are the least hardy of the three species of Thuja referred to here, and need to be well protected from cold winds and frost. Golden and variegated forms especially need full sun.
Soil   A deep, well drained but moist loam that is slightly acid, pH 6.5, is most suitable. The Chinese Arbor-vitae and its varieties resent dry conditions, to which they are sensitive. On poor soils apply a dressing of 70g per sq. m (2oz. per sq. yd) of general fertilizer before planting, and repeat each spring for the first few years.

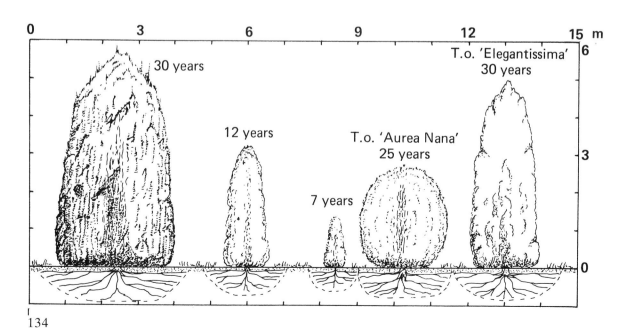

Notes on culture

Planting Plant small conifers, up to 600mm (2ft) high, in late spring or early autumn. Protect those set out in autumn from cold winds and frost, by the use of temporary shelter if need be. Staking and tying is not neccessary. Keep the ground around young plants weed-free, well watered and mulched.

Space Allow each tree or shrub a minimum area equal in diameter to its width at maturity. Avoid planting closer to buildings than two-thirds the expected width when full grown.

Pruning Prune tree forms to limit main shoots to one central leader, and dwarf conifers to keep them in good shape. Beyond that, the less cutting the better.

Plant associations Both small and tall forms look well among other dwarf conifers, or with heathers or rock plants.

Pest and disease control Rarely necessary.

Propagation By seed sown in spring. Named varieties by cuttings taken in late summer or early autumn.

Season of interest	Winter	Spring	Late spring	Summer	Late summer	Autumn
In full leaf				X—————		—X
Autumn colour	——————————			—X		X—
Flowers						
Fruits				X—————		—X
Bark and stem						

The following five characteristics determine to a great extent the amount of attention a specific tree requires.

	When planted	5 years	20 years
Height	600mm	1·5 m	4·5 m
Width	250mm	750mm	2·25 m
Root spread	250mm	1·0 m	3·0 m
Hardiness	C	C	B/C
Wind-firm	3	2/3	2

Plant care profile

	Minimum	Average	High
Site needs		X———X	
Soil needs		X———X	
Pruning		X	
Staking	X		
Maintenance	X———X		

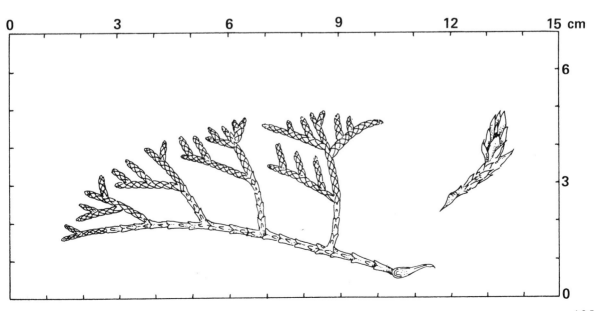

| 0 | 3 | 6 | 9 | 12 | 15 cm |

135

Thuja plicata – CUPRESSACEAE
Giant Arbor-vitae, Western Arbor-vitae, Western Red Cedar

A hardy evergreen tree.
Origin Western North America.

Uses
The Western Red Cedar makes an impressive specimen tree for large gardens, and can also be used for screening and hedging, though in this case some pruning or trimming is necessary. The varieties may be used for the same purposes, and are suitable for both large and medium gardens. The dwarf kinds are excellent singly or in groups, in small gardens or rock gardens.

Description
Dimensions Ultimate size rarely exceeds 18m (60ft) high by 7m (23ft) wide in gardens.
Rate of growth Rapid to moderate.
Life span These conifers can live well over 100 years.
Habit Pyramidal, tapering towards the apex but gradually broadening with age. Isolated single specimens develop broadly pyramidal crowns with large lower branches.
Leaves Scale-like and mid-green.
Flowers Insignificant.
Fruits Cones which are yellowish brown to light brown when ripe, are up to 12mm (½in.) long.

Bark Light brown, and peeling off in strips.

Features
The Western Red Cedar is root- and wind-firm on most soils, and grows well under a fairly wide range of conditions. Under good conditions can be rather vigorous.
Pollution Tolerant.
Non-poisonous.

Varieties
Thuja plicata 'Fastigiata'. A narrow erect-branched form, providing a useful green wall when planted as a screen. In 40 years or so grows to about 12m (40ft) high by 3m (10ft) wide, but can be kept lower by pruning.
Thuja plicata 'Rogersii'. A slow-growing rounded or domed bush, rarely more than 1m (3½ft) high by 1m (3½ft) wide. Foliage golden bronze all the year round.
Thuja plicata 'Stoneham Gold'. Slow-growing dwarf conifer with a broadly pyramidal outline. Leaves scale-like, arranged vertically plate fashion, and dark green with yellow tips.
Thuja plicata 'Zebrina'. Slow-growing, but eventually produces a tall tree, up to 12–15m (40–50ft) high by 6–7.5m (20–25ft)

wide. Foliage light green, splashed yellow, giving an over-all golden effect.

Requirements
Position A sunny but sheltered situation, well protected from cold or dry winds, in an area with a moist mild or cool temperate climate suits these trees.
Soil A deep, well drained but moist loam that is slightly acid, pH 6.5, is most suitable, but these conifers will tolerate alkaline soils. On poor or sandy soils apply a dressing of 70g per sq. m (2oz. per sq. yd) of general fertilizer before planting, and repeat each spring for the first few years.

Notes on culture
Planting Plant small conifers, up to 600mm (2ft) high, in autumn or late spring. Staking and tying is not necessary for small plants, but larger trees need support until firmly rooted. Keep the ground around young plants weed-free, well watered and mulched.
Space Allow each tree or shrub a minimum area equal in diameter to its width at maturity. The true Western Red Cedar should not be grown closer to buildings than 9m

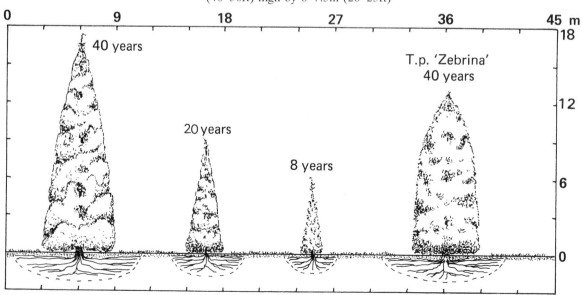

(30ft) unless it is regularly pruned to prevent it from attaining full size. The tall varieties should not be closer to buildings than 6m (20ft) unless they are pruned regularly.

Pruning Prune tree forms to limit main shoots to one central leader. The Western Red Cedar can stand regular clipping, hence its use as hedging. Tree forms can be prevented from further upward growth by removing the growing point just below the required height. On all types cut back damaged, diseased or untidy shoots to maintain a good shape.

Plant associations Useful with other conifers and as background for colourful flowers.

Pest and disease control Honey fungus occasionally attacks these conifers. If planting on land which may have been contaminated, remove all old tree stumps and sterilize the soil with formaldehyde. Allow the fumes to dissipate from the soil before planting; this normally takes four to six weeks. Protect seedlings from leaf blight with fungicide sprays.

Propagation By seed sown by spring. Named varieties by cuttings taken in late summer or early autumn.

Season of interest	Winter	Spring	Late spring	Summer	Late summer	Autumn
In full leaf	X——————————————————————————————X					
Autumn colour						
Flowers						
Fruits					X——————————X	
Bark and stem	X——————————————————————————————X					

The following five characteristics determine to a great extent the amount of attention a specific tree requires.

	When planted	5 years	20 years
Height	600 mm	2·5 m	9·0 m
Width	250 mm	1·5 m	4·0 m
Root spread	250 mm	2·5 m	5·5 m
Hardiness	B/C	B	B
Wind-firm	3	2	1/2

Plant care profile

	Minimum	Average	High
Site needs		X	
Soil needs		X	
Pruning		X——X	
Staking	X		
Maintenance		X——X	

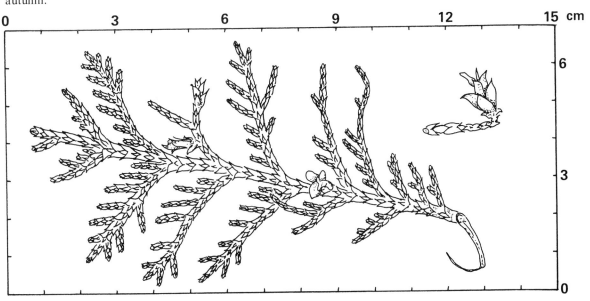

137

Cultivation—a summary chart

Name	Size(m) height	width	Growth rate	Planting season	Planting size
Abies balsamea	9	3	moderate to slow	autumn and late spring	small
Abies concolor	15	4.5	slow to rapid	autumn and late spring	small
Abies delavayi forrestii	12	4.5	rapid to moderate	autumn and late spring	small
Abies koreana	4.5	3	slow	autumn and late spring	small
Abies lasiocarpa	15	7.5	slow	autumn and late spring	small
Abies pinsapo	12	6	moderate to slow	autumn and late spring	small
Calocedrus decurrens	15	2	slow	autumn and late spring	small
Cedrus atlantica	18	7.5	slow to moderate	autumn and late spring	small
Cedrus deodara	18	6	slow to moderate	autumn and late spring	small
Cedrus libani	15	9	slow to moderate	autumn and late spring	small
Cephalotaxus harringtonia	3.5	3	slow	autumn and late spring	small
Chamaecyparis lawsoniana	13.5	4	moderate to rapid	autumn and late spring	small
Chamaecyparis nootkatensis	12	4.5	moderate to rapid	autumn and late spring	small
Chamaecyparis obtusa	12	4	slow	autumn and late spring	small
Chamaecyparis pisifera	10.5	4.5	moderate to slow	autumn and late spring	small
Chamaecyparis thyoides	7.5	3	moderate to slow	autumn and late spring	small
Cryptomeria japonica	15	5	moderate to rapid	autumn and late spring	small
x *Cupressocyparis leylandii*	16.5	6	moderate to rapid	late spring	small
Cupressus glabra	10.5	4.5	moderate to slow	autumn and late spring	small
Ginkgo biloba	10.5	6	moderate to slow	late spring	small
Juniperus chinensis	7.5	2	slow	late summer, early autumn and late spring	small
Juniperus communis	5	2	slow	late summer, early autumn and late spring	small
Juniperus conferta	0.5	4	slow to moderate	late summer, early autumn and late spring	small
Juniperus horizontalis	0.4	4.5	slow to moderate	late summer, early autumn and late spring	small
Juniperus x media	2.5	4	slow to rapid	late summer, early autumn and late spring	small
Juniperus procumbens	0.5	5	slow to moderate	late summer, early autumn and late spring	small
Juniperus recurva	6	3.5	slow	late summer, early autumn and late spring	small
Juniperus sabina	4.5	3	slow to moderate	late summer, early autumn and late spring	small
Juniperus scopulorum	6	2.5	slow to moderate	late summer, early autumn and late spring	small
Juniperus squamata	0.75	2	slow	late summer, early autumn and late spring	small
Juniperus virginiana	9	5	slow to moderate	late summer, early autumn and late spring	small

Hardiness	Maintenance needs	Soil reaction	Site and light requirements
B	average	AN	shelter/ls
B	average	AN	sun and shelter
B	average	AN	shelter/ls
B	low	AN	sun and shelter
A/B	average	AN	sun and shelter/ls
B/C	average	NC	sun and shelter
B/C	low	N	sun and shelter
B/C	high	NC	sun and shelter
C	average	N	sun and shelter
B/C	high	N	sun and shelter
B	low	ANC	shelter/ls
A/B	low	ANC	sun and shelter/ls
A	average	AN	sun/ls
B/C	average	A	sun and shelter
B/C	average	AN	sun and shelter/ls
B/C	low	AN	sun and shelter/ls
B/C	average	A	sun and shelter/ls
A/B	average	ANC	sun/ls
B/C	average	AN	sun and shelter
B/C	average	AN	sun and shelter
B	low	ANC	sun and shelter
A/B	low	ANC	sun/ls
B/C	average	N	sun and shelter/ls
A/B	average	AN	sun and shelter
B/C	average	ANC	sun and shelter
B	average	N	sun and shelter
B/C	average	ANC	sun and shelter/ls
B/C	average	NC	sun and shelter/ls
A/B	low	AN	sun and shelter
B/C	low	AN	sun and shelter
B/C	low	ANC	sun and shelter

Key to chart

Size
  ultimate height and width in
    metres.

Growth rate
  average annual growth
  rapid   = 300mm (1ft)
  moderate = 150–300mm (6in.–1ft)
  slow   = less than 150mm (6in).

Planting season
  when to plant.

Planting size
  ordinary = up to 2.5m (8ft) high.
  small   = up to 1m (3½ft) high.

Hardiness
  A = hardy in cool temperate areas.
  B = hardy in mild temperate areas.
  C = hardy in warm temperate areas.
  Refer to maps on pages 13–14.

Maintenance needs
  high   = above average attention.
  average = average attention.
  low   = minimal care.

Soil reaction
  conifers need or will tolerate
  A = acid soil, pH below 7.
  N = neutral soil, pH 7.
  C = chalky or alkaline soil, pH
    above 7.
  Combinations of letters indicate the
  range tolerated.

Site and light
  requirements
  sun   = a position open to sun.
  shelter = protection from cold or
        strong winds.
  ls   = light shade tolerated.

Continued

Name	Size(m)		Growth rate	Planting season	Planting size
	height	width			
Picea abies	15	6	moderate to rapid	autumn to late spring	small
Picea breweriana	9	5	slow to moderate	autumn to late spring	small
Picea glauca	7.5	2.7	slow	autumn to late spring	small
Picea omorika	15	3	moderate to rapid	autumn to spring	small
Picea orientalis	15	6	slow to moderate	autumn to spring	small
Picea pungens	9	3.5	slow to moderate	autumn to spring	small
Pinus aristata	4	2	slow	autumn to spring	small
Pinus cembra	7.5	3	slow	late summer to autumn	small
Pinus heldreichi leucodermis	9	4.5	slow to moderate	autumn to spring	small
Pinus mugo	4.5	4.5	slow	autumn to spring	small
Pinus nigra	10.5	7.5	moderate to rapid	autumn to spring	small
Pinus parviflora	9	4.5	moderate to slow	autumn to spring	small
Pinus sylvestris	12	5	slow to moderate	autumn to spring	small
Pseudotsuga menziesii	23	6	rapid	autumn to late spring	small
Taxodium distichum	12	5	slow	autumn and late spring	small
Taxus baccata	6	6	moderate to slow	autumn to late spring	small
Thuja occidentalis	9	5	slow to moderate	autumn to late spring	small
Thuja orientalis	6	3.5	slow	autumn and late spring	small
Thuja plicata	18	7	rapid to moderate	autumn and late spring	small

Hardiness	Maintenance needs	Soil reaction	Site and light requirements
A	average	A	sun and shelter/ls
B	average	AN	sun and shelter/ls
A/B	high	A	sun and shelter/ls
A	low	AN	sun and shelter/ls
B	average	A	sun and shelter/ls
A/B	average	AN	sun and shelter/ls
B/C	low	AN	sun and shelter
B	low	A	sun and shelter
A/B	low	ANC	sun
A/B	low	AN	sun and shelter
B	low	ANC	sun and shelter
B/C	low	AN	sun and shelter
A	average	ANC	sun/ls
A/B	average	AN	sun and shelter/ls
B/C	average	ANC	sun and shelter/ls
A	average	ANC	sun and shelter/ls
B/C	average	AN	sun and shelter
C	average	AN	sun and shelter
A/B	high	ANC	sun and shelter

Glossary

Acid   term given to soils which contain little or no calcium, and have a pH level below 7.

Adult foliage   Conifer leaves so described consist of small scales which develop only after plants reach a certain age or stage of maturity. See Juvenile foliage, below.

Alkaline   term given to soils which contain plenty of calcium or other salts and have a pH level above 7. Chalk or alkaline soils are not suitable for plants such as rhododendrons which need acid conditions.

Berry   botanically a small fleshy fruit, usually containing one or more seeds.

Break   plants are said to break when buds start into growth to form shoots.

Catkin   a pendulous flower-spike devoid of petals.

Chlorosis   an ailment of plants characterized by yellowing of leaves, and usually caused by iron deficiency (most common on chalk or alkaline soils).

Columnar   column-like. Trees having near vertical sides with rounded or flattened tops.

Compost   seed or potting compost, intended for growing plants in containers, consists of a balanced mixture of soil, sand and peat or similar plus fertilizer. Compost made from vegetable or plant remains is used as a substitute for farmyard manure.

Cone   the typical fruit of conifers, consisting of woody scales arranged round a central stalk bearing the seeds.

Conifer   term applied to cone-bearing plants or their allies.

Crown   the arrangement of branches of a tree or shrub.

Deciduous   shedding the leaves in winter.

Dormant   in a resting condition, used here with reference to living but leafless trees, shoots and seeds that are not actively growing.

Evergreen   bearing leaves throughout the year.

Fastigiate   tall, narrow and upright in habit with near-vertical branches, applied to trees.

Forking   a condition of trees or shoots in which two or more growths of roughly equal vigour develop from one shoot.

Fungicide   a substance used to control fungus diseases.

Genus   a group consisting of one or a number of botanically similar species. See Species, below.

Glaucous   a term used to describe a greenish or bluish grey colouring on leaves, stems and plants.

Globose   round or spherical in shape.

Grafting   a process of uniting two plants so that one, the rootstock, acts as the roots for the other, the scion.

Ground cover   plants so described are usually low-growing, providing dense ground coverage and smothering weeds, They are often placed below or between trees and shrubs.

Hardy able to grow outside and survive average winters without harm.

Humus a dark brown substance resulting from the decomposition of organic matter. Much valued as a soil improver.

Hybrid the progeny arising from the crossing of two distinct varieties.

Insecticide a substance used to control insect pests.

Juvenile foliage on conifers, awl shaped leaves, usually on young plants and giving way to adult foliage as plants mature. See Adult foliage, above.

Lime a material containing chalk or calcium-rich substances. It is used to neutralize acid soils.

Loam a soil mixture, usually free-draining, which consists of a well balanced blend of clay, sand and organic matter.

Mulch a dressing of manure, peat or similar placed on the soil around plants to conserve moisture during spring and summer.

Neutral neither acid nor alkaline, having a pH level of 7.

Organic matter animal or vegetable matter, used primarily to improve soils. In strict chemical terms this applies to any compound that contains carbon.

pH a scale of measurement used to indicate acidity or alkalinity on which 7 is neutral, numbers above 7 indicate alkalinity, and those below indicate acidity.

Procumbent low-growing, having branches or stems which trail on or just above ground level.

Propagation process by which plants are increased: in the case of conifers normally seeds, cuttings or grafting.

Pyramidal conical in outline, broadening at the base, tapering towards the top.

Rootstock and Scion see Grafting, above.

Shrub a plant having more than one stem at soil level.

Species a group consisting of one or a number of botanically very similar plants. See Genus, above.

Stratification a process in which seeds are subjected to cold and frost to break dormancy and assist germination.

Tree a plant having a woody single or main vertical stem.

Trunk the main stem of a tree above ground level and below the lowest branch.

Underplanting the practice of planting low-growing subjects under or among taller trees and shrubs.

Undercutting a form of root pruning, carried out on conifers a few months before lifting and transplanting to produce a compact root ball.

Weed a plant, usually of little value, growing in the wrong place.

Weeping having pendulous branches or shoots which hang down.

Whorl an arrangement of buds, stems or shoots which originate at the same level, usually in a circle.

Bibliography

Bean, W. J., *Trees and Shrubs Hardy in the British Isles*, vols. I–III, John Murray, London, 1970–76.

Chittenden, F. J. (ed.), *The Royal Horticultural Society Dictionary of Gardening*, Oxford University Press, London, 1956.

Conover, H. S., *Grounds Maintenance Handbook*, McGraw Hill, New York, 1977.

Hay, R. and Beckett, K., *The Reader's Digest Encyclopedia of Garden Plants and Flowers,* Reader's Digest, London, 1975.

Hilliers' Manual of Trees and Shrubs, David and Charles, Newton Abbot, 1974.

Rehder, A., *Manual of Cultivated Trees and Shrubs*, Collier Macmillan, New York, 1940.